KENNETH BERNARD DEAN

THE
BOOK
OF SIX

VOLUME 2

PROCRASTINATIONS
OF THE DAY PAST
NEW EDITION

ISBN: 979-8-89216-029-2 (Paperback)

Library of Congress Control Number: 2024914322

BookmarcAlliance
California, USA
www.bookmarcalliance.com

TABLE OF CONTENTS

PRELUDE

The Book of Six is an open mind share, meant to rekindle that thing inside, which makes us both humanly open to or curiously in search of the truth. Volume 2: "Procrastinations of the day past," is just that! Procrastinations and Daydreams that perhaps even you have or might contemplate, once you've read the contents of the eight pieces totaling about 28,316 words, which I have chosen to release at this point and now. So, without further ado, I give you "The Book of SIX Volume 2: Procrastinations of the day past" by Kenneth Bernard Dean/LDD/Six. The first story titled, "Forever the Night" is a 4,118 word short story of an interplanetary invasion and the location of the experience is set in Saint Paul Minnesota. It tells the story of how one man and his small family, took it upon themselves to make a stand at any cost towards defending their right to exist in the Universe. Nonetheless, (in many ways) perhaps even you've entertained same or similar procrastinations as well, do you not think or believe it to be so? The second story is one of imagination, which also puts humanity in a fight for their right to exist in this vast Universe.

The name is "Forward to Delta" and it is a 5,471 word story set to make the experience, one filled with looking at the negative attributes, which, I'm sure, will resonate within you the reader, Thus, giving you that same feeling of what it must feel like, to be under the watchful eyes of the planetary community in which we [Earth] are being watch by. This is a wake-up call for the people of this world, to fight for both Earth and Humanity right of existence within the Universe location of the "Delta Quadrant!" Next, we come to the third story title "My Death, My Life One in the same" is a 1,473 word question of our purpose of existence. Plus, I know that it will leave you asking yourself some of those same questions. The forth story is titled "Survivors of the Wrath" a short 2,230 word story of what it might be like, for man to go forth and retaliate against their alien attacker, by invading their world. It also gives some slight feel to what might be the mindset once the aggression is over and the planetary coexistence began. Now, the fifth story is one which tells a story of man opportunity to venture far back before the Idea of God or the true beginning of time itself. Though it is just a thought, I believe for the openminded reader this will prove to be a fine read. Number six of the stories is called "The Elephant in the Room" which is a 2,198 word short story which I think you'll enjoy. For it is the story about this, though unseen, still tangible beast that for far too long has been in control of this negative destiny through life, which Humanity has so chosen. It also speaks of a possible solution (maybe) to the said problem. So, with that all being said, I only ask that you, while reading the material, please do it with an open mind. Then there is story number seven titled "The Paradox of the Empathetic Entity" a 2,170 word story of what it must have been like for the Lord God Almighty, to within itself except both his decision of creation, as well as himself after the fact. And the final story is titled "Though I stand, Still I've Yet to learn how to Walk" this is a 4,200 word short story that speaks about the two basic stimuli, Faith and Pride, which motivates our choice option in life. This piece explores a few levels, where choice is a major factor in our everyday life. I'm sure that you (the reader) will find it to be a mind opening experience, one I'm sure you will enjoy.

Also, I ask that if you find that the material is appealing to your sense of curiosity, and question of what is or is not the truth, and you want more then contact me by way of my email address and let me direct you where you can find more of my books to stimulate the curiosity which lie within your need to appease your open-mindedness. Again, thank you, and like always the hope is that you enjoy.

Thank you,
Kenneth Bernard Dean/LDD/Six
forwardtodelta@yahoo.com

CHAPTER I

Forever the Night

~A Word from the Author~

E
ven though it may seem to have happened fast, I can still remember when it first became known that both they existed and that they were on their way here. One could have only imagined what might be in store for us. However, no one could have imagined anything so horribly vial as this would follow in the aftermath of their arrival to our home world, Earth.

Though some might speculate that had it not been for the many space launches, which were of military priority, then maybe the wrath that is upon us would not be. However, this somehow seems to be of little importance, considering these creatures, and the veracity of their attack on both the Planet and its' human resource, us...

Thus, I ask that you (the reader) once again experience another moment in "The Mind of Insanity" along with me. Who knows, perhaps you have had the same or similar thoughts as well. So, to you, and with no further ado, I give you the piece titled "Forever the Night." For it is designed to allow you to (at least) feel comfortable with your thoughts while experiencing a similar concept from someone else.

However, the hope is that the experience you will enjoy. As always, thank you for both your interest and your support.

FOREVER THE NIGHT

Chapter 1: Day One or Monday

I *can still remember those days of the past, whereupon diversity was our biggest divergent to world unity and peace. However, the day they came, all those ideas went right out the window. For in the real, there was no place for our petty problems, which we founded in our ethnicity and cultural differences as being the problem. Because these alien people from afar did more towards unifying humanity (the World over), by just coming here, than we could have achieved, even if we put more effort, and more time, "like about, another four hundred years or so, into it!" And in opposition to all the politics, and marches ever! For the fight that we are in is one of survival and for the right to exist.*

As I can recall, it was about 11:45 a.m., when first they appeared in our skies on that cold and winter morning in Saint Paul, MN. Yet one could only imagine the purpose of their coming. When suddenly, and without provocation or threat, they began to attack. As we watched areas the size of full blocks, being destroyed by what seemed to be some kind of laser pulse weapon.

As I watched the death and destruction occurring all around me, the thought of my two young grandsons, who were attending school not too far away, came to mind. And I became both scared and angry over the fear, which must have been going through their young minds.

Now, the only thoughts that I had in mind were acquiring a car, a gun, and collecting all my family or at least those I could get too, and fast! When out the side of my view, I caught a glimpse of a truck sitting in the middle of the road, with both doors open and the engine still running. So, without even thinking, I jumped in and headed towards the school since it was closer.

As I drove through the streets, which was now reduced to a collection of vehicles, some with occupants, others empty though the engine was still running, I began to call my older grandson to let him know both that I was coming to get him, and to check on his welfare as well.

As he answered, though being scared, he managed to assure me that for the moment, all was okay with him. Thus, a sign of relief swept over me as I hung up that call and tried to contact other members of my small family while still proceeding towards the school.

Within an hour, the view of the school, about a block away, came into sight. Understand, on any typical day, that same trip would take at the worst, maybe twenty minutes. However, this was no typical or ordinary day, and without even thinking, I pulled the truck up onto someone's front yard. Then began to run the rest of the way to the school, searching for my boys' as I made it to the school's main entrance. I wasted no time, as I ripped the door open. Then began searching for my boys among the many scared children there, as they too, were waiting for someone to come for them as well. When in the distance, I could hear their voices calling out to me, *"Grandfather, we're over here! Here Grandfather, over here!"*

Now, I must say upon hearing their voices, was like the Lord was there all the time, just protecting them long enough for me or someone in the family to come and collect them. However, there was no time for celebration. For there were still others, to be both collected as well as contacted. You know, to check their welfare as well. So, without even a second thought, I scooped them both up and headed back towards the truck. As we prepared to pull out of the front yard, a small craft from one of the larger ships came overhead and began to level the school and most of that same block.

Thus, without hesitation, I threw the truck into reverse and floored it into the street. Then I slammed it into forward-drive, and with wheels spinning and smoking, I headed toward downtown Saint Paul to collect another of my grandsons. When like the Fourth of July, the skies over downtown Saint Paul lit up from explosions occurring from a main crafts' attack on this metropolitan mainstay.

Seeing this caused my heart to sink, for I could only fear for my grandsons' safety during this grave time in the history of humanity's existence. When right in front of me, I could see him moving in the rush of people. Who they, themselves, were seeking safety away from the area of destruction and violence that was going on behind them.

Thus, I stirred the truck in his direction. Hoping and seeking to cut him off and pick him up in the truck. Then find perhaps a safer place to try and regroup. While at the same time, he, and I both (with our cell phones) would attempt to contact the other family members, yet unheard from at that point. Thus, like clockwork, it came to be, and within minutes, he also was among the truck's safety. As we made it back to what once was the building complex I lived in, it was plain to see that there was not much left.

However, there was pretty much most of the center of the complex still intact. And as luck would have it, my apartment was one of those spared from the attack. So, without hesitation, we took the stairs up three floors of open stairway, and soon we were in the safety of four walls, a ceiling, and a door.

While my oldest grandson and I made calls to the missing family members, I couldn't help looking out the window and seeing the damage and debris lying out before me and again thinking: *"What could have brought this type of wrath upon us? Like really, what could we have done that was so wrong, to warrant this kind of reprisal!"....*

Somehow, in the midst of it all, the youngest grandson of mine looked up into my eyes and asked, *"if I had contacted any other family members yet?"* Looking down into his face, while trying to make sense of it all, the only words that came to me at the time was, *"don't worry, we are all going to be fine."* Then I gave him the task of covering all the windows with tape and newspaper. Then handing a spare cell phone to the other slightly older grandson, I then directed him to call his grandmother.

At about that time, the oldest grandson came into the room with his mother on the phone and handed it to me. I told my daughter after she assured me, though being a little bruised; still, she was both okay and halfway to my House, how relieved I was to hear that she was okay and on her way to my house. Then she asked if I had heard from any of the others, most specifically her mom. I replied no, not at that moment. However, though once I hung up from her, I was going to continue to try to make contact starting with her mom first. Then no sooner she hung up, the phone rang ever so quickly. Answering, it became clear that it was her mom, who informed me that she had talked to both our sons and that they, and their prospective families, were in route to my home and should arrive perhaps within the hour.

Thus, within an hour and forty-five minutes, we were all once again together, and now the business at hand was first to reach out to the other family members, both locally and nationwide, as we put together a list of those who survived, those missing, and those who were lost to the first attack. Though it was very hard thinking about it and remembering those so suddenly ripped from us by these warriors from afar, it was still a thing which had to be done, just for accountability alone.

Now, with that being done, both of my sons began to contact friends of theirs, you know, friends who were gang-members, some Crip's others Vice Lord's. Also, as the reports came over KMOJ, a Minneapolis based radio station, it became quite grim in the reporting that all Major Capital Cities and Control Centers, be it Local or National Capitals' the World over, had either been destroyed or were at that time under attack, when the order to break into Gun stores and Pawnshops were ordered or given that at least some might have a fighting chance, and possibly battle hard enough to create a buffer or DMZ type of line between both ourselves, and our alien attackers. When some critical breaking news took president, over all reports thus far, and it started with the statement: *"As of the last five minutes, we have received a report, both President Trump and VP Pence are dead!!"*

The report went on further to say, along with both the President and his VP, both the House of Congress members and the House of the Senate members were also killed during that same attack on the Capitol Hill in Washington, DC. It went on further to say the attack happened while they were all in an emergency meeting over and about the now alien problem when it all occurred.

Now for many, here in the United States of America. That will go down in their minds, as perhaps the one good thing they, "these Alien Bastards" could have done for Earth's people. However, their attack overshadowed it, and soon we were back to the reality at hand, the existence of our survival! The room was soon filled with activity. Every working cell phone was being pushed to its maximum in performance as the room itself took on the appearance of a major military war room or Intel-collection point. For with the help of both my sons and my nephew Paul, we were able to gather the troops in a sense and put together a [somewhat] formidable fighting force, as they and their families came, and joined forces with ours. The women and children constituted the support and medical backbone of this fighting force.

Before long, we began to transform the remainder of the complex into a formidable fighting outpost as we cleared and cleaned up the debris and the bodies tossed about during the first attack. Before long, and by the close of the day, you could see the progress as we placed overwatch positions throughout the building. Then, while moving all essentials (food, medical, water, extra weapons, and such) to the basement, it became quite clear that our clean water supply was too small to sustain (at the least), the force we already had.

So we sent out patrols looking for both other survivors and other supplies (guns and ammo, food, and medicine), but most importantly, "clean water." For it is a known fact, man does not live by bread alone. But that the body can live longer with water then it can without. Plus, it would be good to know that we had an adequate supply before putting together a formidable attack plan for dealing with these alien bastards' from outer space!! Suddenly, like a miracle from heaven, we happened upon a whole eighteen-wheel truck full of it. As both my sons climbed into the cab, I told them to fire it up. Thus, the sounds of a big heavy-duty diesel engine cranked on like clockwork. Just that sound alone, like music to my ears, was all the reassurance I needed, and boy was that not a very good feeling.

"I mean, considering our present situation!" Well, whatever the case, the moment of celebration soon came to an end as I directed them both to return to the compound with that miracle truck of water. With the remainder of the party, I continued on searching for both additional supplies and any information that could or would assist us in eradicating these alien invaders from afar from our home-world Earth! As we moved through the night across an open field, now bath in the night moon's fluorescent light. It became very real that though today was Monday, perhaps by maybe Saturday or even next Monday, we might not exist. So, what would be the purpose of continuing this hopeless or pointless endeavor, if (in fact) that well may be the case. "But then I say to myself, so what if that is the case, at the least one thing is for sure, we will not go away without taking a lot of them with us, so have at it you alien assholes!!" For, this World belongs to us alone, and judging from those around me, it was plain to see they too felt the same. "So bring it, you unearthly bastards, because we're ready!!"

However, the black of the night soon gave way to the light of the morning sun as we soon returned to the compound, both tired and hungry. However, the coming sleep was the one luxury I most looked forward to, as I entered what once was my apartment alone. Again no one could have imagined what was to come with the dawn of that second day.

FOREVER THE NIGHT

Chapter 2: "Wake-up, wake-up, they're coming!!"

*A*ll I know is that I am a boxer, and my job is to knock the other guy's ass out before he does me. "Okay, champ, are you ready for this because I can tell you the guy in the next room certainly is, and I hate to say it. But he does not mind going through you, just to get the title of heavyweight champion of the World do you hear me. So, let me see your "war face," let me hear you scream loud enough to make him shit in his pants. Come-on! Scream!!"

"Get up, get up fast!" For its time, and they are coming in both a large-scale air and ground assault! Okay, I'm up! I'm up! Is everyone ready? Are the children all safe, and in the basement? Yes, and we are as prepared as we will be, and may the Lord bless us this day with either a victory or a swift death. Well, either way, make sure that there are enough ammo and water at every battle station, and remember, keep it coming!

For I have a feeling, this will be, in a sense, our longest day. So, let us make ready to defend both our families and our home planet Earth. Now, with a pair of binoculars, I could see the advancement of their ground forces while overhead, the skies were filled with aircraft from all over the World in battle with these alien bastards sky-crafts from afar. When suddenly their ground forces came within range of our murderous fire! Then it started: *"Hurry! Some more ammo! Look, it's getting a little thick out there!"* Then it happened, and what an injury it was.

Like somebody took a red-hot knife and peeled the skin right off, and straight down to the bone. Sad to say, but this was someone who came to us seeking to avenge the wrong brought on Earth and his loved ones by these bastards of afar. Will he survive, one only knows. However, there is no time for thinking about that for the time now is for killing, and right now, that is all that is on or in my mind, *"Killing!"* As I pan my viewpoint to the left, it was plain to see that their right flank had all but broken through. So, I gave the order to strengthen the left side of our lines, with the reserves, in the hope of holding the defensive line there, long enough to start a full-scale fallback of our nonessential personal to a more safer position.

Once that had been achieved, I then gave the order too fallback to our next prepared line of defense, as we fought and died the whole way there as I posed the question: *"Are we in position yet? Then let the bastards have it!"* And with that being said, a switch was triggered, and our earlier positions went up like the 4th of July. *"Have at it, you alien bastards. You wanted it, and now you have it! Enjoy the Bar-B-Q, you fuckers!!"* As the fire rose high into the sky, along with the smoke. I felt a sense of victory, as the stench of their burning corpse filled my nostrils and caused my eyes to water from its acidic effects. Soon it was time to collect up our wounded and bury our dead. I guess that was the hardest part of it all, for though no family members of mine were among them. The fact that they were of Earth still brought tears rushing down my face in honor of their sacrifice for this, our home-world Earth! Moreover, in that moment of sorrow, we all pledged that whatever the cost and no matter the amount of time. We would do whatever it took to take back our Planet from these invading bastards from afar!

Before long, the night was again upon us, as we sifted through the night looking for any signs of a possible counterattack. When suddenly lights, and I mean a lot of lights, were heading right for us: *"What do you think is happening?"* Is a question someone asked. *"I do not know, but whatever it is, we better be ready!"* Was the answer I gave. For in that moment, I was both scared and without answers though the lights kept coming. Knowing that this may well be our final moment, I gave the word to prepare for the worst. As all able-bodied men, women, and children alike readied themselves for what we thought was possibly our last night on Earth. When suddenly, someone asked: *"Do aliens know how to drive cars?"* Now hearing this caused a slight to ponder to occur, as I wondered while watching these lights closely, as they came ever so close: *"Is it true, can aliens really drive a car?"* Then about fifty yards out, the lights came to an abrupt stop! As figures resembling humanoids started to come out of them and head in our direction. Yet, because of the smoke and haze of the earlier battle, it was somewhat difficult to determine whether they were human or alien.

"Steady, everyone hold your fire! Hold on! Hold!" Then like a dream come true, they turned out to be human. Troops from the *Red Bull Division of Minnesota's National Guards*, indeed, a God-sent answer to our lost hopes and needs. As they came closer, I could hear them asking how many us there were and if we were all okay. As we came out from behind our defensive positions, it was understandable for them to see that we indeed had been in a battle. *"Man, are we glad to see you guys." "Yeah, it is a good thing that we saw the skies lit up on the horizon. Hell! We thought that everyone in this sector was either dead or gone by now." "However, it looks like if you guys were not here, we probably would not have been able to evacuate all the hospitals in this sector. So, you can all consider yourselves, heroes in a real sense..." "Truly, I can see from all these alien bodies all over that you had yourselves one hell of a night. However, our orders are to get you all to the safe zone for hot food, showers, and debriefings; Okay?"*

Then I turned to the officer in charge and asked if he did not mind loading our injured first, and he nodded okay as we started to bring them forward. Looking back now, it was plain to me that had it not been for all our will to survive, we, as well as all those in the many hospitals in our area, would, for lack of a better word, have been lost in those first two days of the invasion thus, as we carried our wounded to the trucks that awaited us. We did it amidst the loud claps and cheers of the troops, which bordered our way there. However, looking back, we must have looked like hell, but a proud hell in a sense. For like he said, we were all true heroes. Nonetheless, though it has been three years since they first came to our beloved World, Earth, all things seem to be going in the right direction. The ideas that once surrounded our hearts and minds, like a dark cloud of hate for our fellow human race, are no longer there. Why? Because we have finally realized that for our specie to exist, we must learn to live together as one people. That being, the real people of Earth and, in a sense, I believe that is what the Lord God's purpose was for their coming. That being, the final coming together of one of his most prized creations, "Man."

Anyhow, as the sun recedes over the horizon, the warning goes out over the camp speakers, alerting that it is time for all nonmilitary personal to head for shelter, for that is the time they usually attack. However, I await the day when they are finally defeated. Thus, marking once again, a time when we can again walk among night time, as we gaze up into the star-filled skies of black velvet, no longer afraid of what might be waiting around that next corner. However, till such time, remember to at least stay alive long enough to be a part of the coming victory celebrations. Because I hear, they are going to be off the chain, so keep your head down, and your powder dry and until that day, peace!

~FOOTNOTE~

Truth being, though, this is just another story from "the mind of insanity." The fact still remains, the possibilities of something of this magnitude is still viable. However, as you think about it, do we really need something of this scale or volume to occur before we decide to pull our heads out of our ass and do what it takes to put right this humanity the World over. I mean, it should not take a mass interplanetary invasion for us to come together as the dominant caretakers of this World, Earth. I guess to start; we should begin with the embracing of the gift of diversity. For that in itself, is where humanity begins, and the bullshit stops!

Look, how about you just consider the story you have just read and ponder it for just a moment? Take a look around at the society we have so built for ourselves, and perhaps then you will understand the purpose of this piece. Till next time, here is look in at you from out there. Again, thank you for your time, and like always, the hope is that you both enjoyed it and took from it something of importance to ponder later.

(Just a question: From the Book of Six)
Kenneth Bernard Dean/LDD/Six (-Author)

CHAPTER 2

Forward to Delta

~A Word from the Author~

This piece that you are about to indulge is one that is meant to breed a sense of thought on the subject of, are you alone among the stars of the Universe.

It also comes from many hours of thought on this subject as well. True this concept, is one that has been a part of MANS thoughts, for as long back through time as when both man and woman alike fixed their eyes to the heavens and, in their first language, asked the question, "What is out there among those lights?" So in that memory along, this piece is written.

It has been the destiny handed down to Man by the Creator that Man shall find the answer to that one question one day. The one question which even supersedes that other one, which is "WHERE DO WE GO TO FROM HERE?" Thus some thousands of years later, they find themselves at the doorsteps of that answer of "ARE WE ALONE?"

Now, keep in mind that you might not be able to distinguish thought from reality at times. Thus, this is meant, for it keeps the reader focused on the question of the other life existence among the "Stars of the Universe." So with no further ado, I give you "FORWARD TO DELTA," and as always, I hope that you will enjoy it.

FORWARD TO DELTA

Chapter 1: The truth, the whole truth,
and nothing but

There comes that time when even an entity likened to me feels the need to come clean with the truth, even if no one believes it. I mean, in a way, that is the only perk that this job allows. That being (the fact that) even the truth is beyond belief, is the very thing that protects both myself, as well as the truth itself.

Today is a day of remembrance for one of the worst terror attacks to hit these shores since the Pearl Harbor attack on December 7th, 1941. But (though it is) the thoughts that plague my mind are the same as when man first raised his eyes to the heavens and asked the question, *"Is there anyone out there among the stars of the Universe or Am I along here among the many lights of this vast Universe?"* I mean, I am happy being here on this planet looking up at the lights among this vast heaven. But I am missing out on one of the most extraordinary explorations of man. That being the hunt for other life among the cosmos, and the answer to the question, *"How do they (man) fit among them?"*

Then the reality sets in, as I survey the activities of man's societies the world over. *At that moment alone, even more profound questions surface like, "Are they ready for what they might find?"* Then there is my favorite, *"How will they be accepted in the hearts, mind, and eyes of the many others that do exist throughout the Universe?"*

Now, though these latter questions may sound cynical, they are not meant to discourage any opportunities of man or the quest of humanity out among the Stars of this vast Universe. But these questions must be considered as well. I mean, when you look at what it is that man has accomplished, and in the time, humanity has been on the surface of this world. Well, I must say it reads like something from a book of hate, horror, and deception.

Let us see; you will find that they are good at destroying each other, and equally good at keeping that chaos and destruction alive, with the distaste for the hate that they have so been or grown accustomed to harboring in their hearts against one another. I mean, look, with that kind of resume, I think that it would be safe to say; I do not believe that they (the other worlds) would be thrilled of man coming to their homeworld. In fact, I think that they would do all they could, just to protect themselves from them. Moreover, even to the point of violence and the first strike against them if need be.

Now when you take all that into context, and then watch a movie like *"THE DAY THE EARTH STOOD STILL, INDEPENDENCE DAY, and ARTIFICIAL INTELLIGENCE (A.I.)"* just to name a few. Even you can understand why it is so essential that man works hard at repairing the ills of their own societies the world over or plan not to go anywhere in the Universe hoping to find new life.

"Why should they go looking for life, when they don't even respect most of the life forms, including the human life forms that co-exist here on their own homeworld?"

I mean, (face it) for that should be the real question asked, don't you think? Moreover, man has a lot of internal work, which must be done before they can ever show their face to the rest of the life forms, which may contact them out there. Like a bacterium, they (man) has soiled the existence of a world time had created and put aside just for them along with any who should ever come to visit it.

But I say again openly that like bacteria, they have trained themselves to the design of self-destruction in the sense of seeking world peace. How ironic to think this can ever be, less they destroy every human being that exists here, on such a delicate and most beautiful planet. Somehow in their quest to find or build that perfect dream world, they (rather than moving forward) have resorted to that old way of carnage and self-destruction. In a sense, it is forcing them back to times in their own history when the law of the planet was, *"To kill or to be killed," but this time, it is not for survival. It is for "Personal National Pride, Land Grabbing Schemes, and the control over all-Natural Resources."* Now I ask you if you were sitting up there on a world out in the vast Universe, and just by chance, you were able to catch a glimpse of the chaos and turmoil that is the way of this world's social structure, well need I say more?

Even you would not want to have any contact or dealings with these beings. I guess what it is that I am trying to convey is that time is running out, and before you know it, they are going to come. *Either baring the olive branch of Peace and Prosperity or weapons of actual destruction, they will come. For, the way they see you is the way they perceive your need to be destroyed, totally, and completely.* You know, I guess they were right, those who sit among the council of creation for the Universe, when they said that you were doomed from the start. You know, like back when the man took it upon himself, to speak that first lie into the face of his blessed Creator, for which he was run up out of Eden and told to find his own way from then on. *Now in that time, I believe that man's anger got the best of him; thus, he then forced his hand upon his brethren and sister, then later the children thereof.*

This fact, even you can see every day, through the media's technology. Moreover, you broadcast it everywhere, and every day the world over, likened to that of significant and positively historical accomplishments made by man. I mean, no one can escape the madness which you have brought upon yourselves. Now, to think that you are willing to take that with you, and out to the rest of the Universe, is quite appalling and to the sense of actually being hilarious.

Look, you have a moral responsibility to the human entity you represent on this small planet, and to the rest of the life forms that co-exist alongside you in this world. It is your job to do whatever it takes (short of mass destruction) to bring man to that point in history evolution, where you can say without doubt *"WELCOME"* to those who may come to your world. Also, man must be able to guarantee to all that live here that through their dedication for peace, prosperity, religious belief, and positive technological advancements that their opportunities are beyond their wildest dreams for a better future.

Thus when they do come (those other life forms that is), they will find many species of intelligent and well-evolved life forms still co-existing here on this blue world called Earth. Yes, many species of loving and caring life forms, which incorporate all that love and care into the life forms that live on this world towards a fruitful existence. Moreover, a world of species with that one dream in mind, the goal of spreading out as representatives of Earth among the Universe and advancing their ideas and knowledge through shared technology as a primary cultural exchange program.

FORWARD TO DELTA

Chapter 2: The leaving of the comfort zone of the caves

(for man) is a brighter Horizon

*T*here was once a cave dweller, who after living a majority of his life within the confounds of the cave, and like so many generations before him. He decided to venture out and to see what lay beyond his known Universe.

So as he walked out into that world abroad, he was astounded by what had be-felled his view. For what he had discovered was a world of incredible and unimaginable vastness. One that would prove to be a world of great wonder. A world that would both bring forth great questions, as well as the answers to those questions which had somehow been lying dormant within his mind.

A world of challenges and dreams, where a man or a woman can grow into perfection from all they would acquire, from the knowledge that surrounded them; thus, as this being stood before the vastness of a body of water, which span far beyond the horizons of his view. The urge of exploration grew ever so strong in him, till such a time as several days later, he took to his impulses never to return to those caves ever again.

There comes a time when man will venture out among the stars, just like when he took that first step away from the caves, which he had become so comfortable with. Thus, it will be his first step towards a brighter future in his evolutionary process. But the question is not, *"When or Why?"* For it is embedded in the structure of his DNA that these things shall occur, no question at all. But will he be able to adapt to the many changes that must be before he loses focus on what is really at stake? You know, things like growth in the knowledge of his spiritual being, and his place in the Universe overall. Somewhat like, *"WHO AM I, WHY AM I, and WHERE DO I GO TO FROM HERE?"* Plus, the big one, which comes with living in a Universe so vast that being, *"ARE WE TRULY ALONE?"*

To imagine what it must have been like, for the first man and woman to venture out away from those caves in the beginning, is like beyond any of your modern man comprehension, or is it? For like them, you are now preparing for a similar journey. But this one is set for the stars, and out among the heavens of the Universe.

Thus, like that earlier expedition, it promises both excitements of a wealth of knowledge and dangers, no questions asked. However, two words come to mind about what drives you, and they are: *"Curiosity"* and *"Observation."* Why these words? Because these are the same words that brought you out of the caves and, for a while, taught you and gave purpose to everything that was needed to get you through thus far.

Well, at least until your arrogance came into play, yes, *"Arrogance!!"* A word that, in its very nature, breeds destruction, plus for those who are deceived by the nature of this word, will soon fall prey to the *"Self-Destructive"* properties that it holds. Now multiply that by the numbers of a world's population, like the one here on Earth. "Then, and only then can you (as a person) see how far back in your evolutionary process, you have regressed, thus need I say more?"

"For everything that you are, has come from the spark lit by those two words, Curiosity, and Observation." They taught you what to eat, what to wear, where to live, and a bunch of other qualities that sheltered and made you the beings that you are today. But here you are today, allowing another word, *"Arrogance,"* to send you self destructively backward down a road of no return. Indeed man is a specie; hellbent on losing their focus, as well as any future of existence for all time.

Thus once again, you proudly appeal to this same word to take with you into the communities of the Universe, frantically seeking out and hoping to find life forms, to impose this same *"Arrogance"* upon, and in the hopes of being accepting or even welcomed among them.

But there is an old fact, which has stood the test of time, and before the existence of even the man concept to which it states: *"You get what you bring, nothing more, and nothing less, just simply that!"* So, what makes you think now (especially during your backward slide period) that such things are going to change?

You know, the kind of change that comes with "forward positive motion or movement." Look, either by force or choice, change is something that has to be, or life (as you know it) is no more. Plus, there is no better time than now to implement it into reality. Even logic directs (that) you always put the best out front.

"Why, you might ask?" Because then you are received more peacefully. Therefore, allowing you to make any or all changes towards making the situation more palatable for others. So why then, without correcting themselves first, they are so hell-bent in showing that character flaw to the rest of the Universe, and in the name of the Lord who created everything with just three words which are, *"Let there be!"*

In the Dictionary, the description for the word "MAN" should read: 'Man, one hell-bent on self-destruction, one full of deception, a deceiving entity or a truly evil one.' Now really, take a look at the world around you. For then, and only then, will you be able to understand what is being conveyed in the piece that you are reading. It is time that you put those little ideas of the *"Small Minded Leaders"* that rule the many tracks of surface lands to the side and decide the course of your planet from a socially civilized manner.

One which includes the spiritual aspect of all sides and does what it is that you were created for. *That being, to prepare yourselves to evolve full mind, body, and soul to that level of perfection, which will show the real miracle of the Lord's creative genius, and by way of the "Hebrew Design" point of view or concept from which, your idea came or derived from.*

So, what will it take? Of course, everyone has their theory of what it will take. But the truth is always that, *"The truth!"* So, let me enlighten you to the solution, which is the truth, not to allow you to continue down that path of total self-destruction. The first thing is, you have to believe in what it is that I am about to tell you, and that is simply *"this is a can-do thing,"* then put all aggression the world over on hold.

The next thing is to drop down on your knees, and re-pledge your loyalty, faith, and life to that master of *"Hebrew Design,"* the Almighty Himself. Also, you have to commit to the truth that diversity breeds respect, and the longevity of life and a wealth of great knowledge.

The reason for that last statement can be found within this solar system and is the ultimate punishment for not heeding this advice given. Plus, you can see through a telescope the results for not heeding the warning issued, you know it to be called the *"Asteroid Belt."*

But what it was prior, was no different than Earth and the children thereof were no different from you here on this world Earth. *For a more in-depth truth, you would have to go further and settle the formula of the percentage of melon (natural sunblock) in the DNA structure required for each planet, which orbits your nuclear reactor known to you to be the sun.*

It is true that I could give you the answer, but then I would also control you as well. *"For, whoever controls the knowledge, they to control the people."* Why? Because in all actuality, the truth is human beings live their lives like sheep, and under the guidance of their chosen leaders. Who are mere men like you, and not liken to me who they should pledge their loyalty to. For they also compare themselves to that of GODS. Yet, they are only mere men or, in a sense, great deceivers. Is it not a little ironic (in a sense) that you have not even come to except who or what you really are compared to what truly is?

Even though I know that you are trying hard to follow, still, if nothing else, please ponder what I am about to say. Because I think that it will help, and I believe that you indeed should. Okay, look at where you are located now in the Universe, for it is the *"Alpha Quadrant."* But where you were considered or conceived in the form of a concept is known to be called the *"Delta Quadrant."*

"Why Delta because that is where all things Hebrew come from. Look! To think is to create, and from the beginning, it was only the

Almighty, who had that kind of power." But then, because of his great love for his creation (humanoids), the Lord gave us the entire gift, but with limits attached to it, thus making us all lesser Gods. There is no end to the abilities of this, the greatest gift ever given over to a man.

For, even though the human mind in itself is endlessly eternal, it is nothing like that of our Creator or the vastness of the Universe that his word spoke into being before us all. Now, for this Great Creator to give us that power to create (though with limitations attached to it), it still created a form of sibling rivalry among those greater Gods. Thus, our Creator (God Almighty) placed us here in the *"Alpha Quadrant"* to protect us all from his rivals and has never left us to the wayside as the other creator Gods had done to their creations.

No, our Creator always had faith even in you. Thus the reason for me, now do you understand what that is or truly means? It is known as "A true love for a great idea" concept. Whose ideas? The ideas of a Hebrew Creator, the views of our God. Thus, the only point that he was revealing to you was what it was, and it was Hebrew by design.

Even though it is hard to stomach that there are still those who do not appreciate (the fact) that all things throughout this *"Alpha Quadrant,"* which is of his spoken word concept or upon this world, are Hebrew is mind-boggling! For the fact remains that that is why you say, *"Hebrew God."* I mean, it was not God who turned away from you; it was you who turned from him, and because of that same word, *"Arrogance."* It is indeed time for man to stand up and face it, then except, and repent or reap the benefits of his deceptive and lying ways.

You see, it is okay that you should find humor in what it is that I am saying. But with the truth being told that we are the same, whether we come from this system or one far, far away is really not so funny after all. For, the whole of our existence universally is inner twined.

So what you do here in this world indeed affects the whole in the sum of the big picture. Thus, our Lord (the true Deity) places some among others to bear witness to the flaws in this mass concept of a project; and scribe or record their findings. Thus, again people liken to me come from a great distance to bear witness and record the activity. Therefore, the question then should be, *"So, why are they looking elsewhere, Lord?" For do not, they know, the salvation that they seek, lay among the choices they make. And the fact that it affects us all, less they make a change, we are all doomed for Eternity for those choices."*

You see, that is the talk among the circle of the Planetary Communities throughout the Universe. That this thing (change) come to be, and for the salvation of the rest within this Universal Community. Look, the Lord, who is both of our Deity, is fighting hard not to do what he somehow feel must be done, and that is to remove this blemish called Earth, and all those upon it from further existence.

For like it is written, *"Less you remove the spoiled fruit, given time the rest of the fruit in the barrow shell parish as well!"* Thus, then, and only then, will I finally be allowed to return home once again. For home is where the heart is, and oh how I yearn for my heart. Though even that in itself, to me, seems selfish, I was asked to be here in a sense and to do a job. Even though I still yearn to be on that world of peace and unity, the place I know to be home.

You see, we have been coming here since before you were even considered. We grew the gardens and cared for the other living entities, which you so call animals or beasts of burden. Moreover, it was all done in the preparation of the Lord's next great thing or idea, which in fact, was and is you. Thus, the Lord, the Deity gave conscious to you, and with the two other things that he gave very few others, he gave unto you. That being a soul and the option of choice. That is something that he only granted to a few of us, yet you chose to abuse it and with it yourselves as well. Do not be deceived, for the date 12/21/2012 is only the start of a crucial choice that must be made, and by you alone. Yes, what happens from this day forward comes either with blessings or consequences. Nonetheless, understand to exist in the *"Quadrant of Delta,"* one must be able to endure and evolve truly a positive evolution. Even your negative must be positive by design, just to get you from the *"Alpha Quadrant, forward to Delta."*

FORWARD TO DELTA

Chapter 3: Today, the date read 12/22/2012

The date read 12/22/2012 on the top of the newspaper, held by the man next to me on the train platform. It further went on to say that perhaps the Mayans really did not know what they were saying or doing when they made such a prophecy of possible future events. I mean, just looking around and visualizing the ignorance of modern man was genuinely overwhelming.

But, when I fixed my eyes to the northern heavens, it was indeed plain what lay ahead for the sleeping modern man. I mean, even their crafts of war were somehow soothing to the view as they entered into the skies of this, the world of the Modern Man this world Earth. For, I knew at that moment that he would have to put pride to the wayside, and except the wisdom of the elders, be it Old Mayan, Old Roman, Old Greek, or even the knowledge and wisdom of my people, The Children of the Stars.

Like the great chariots of fire, spoken of in The Book of Revelations, they continued to come. For the Mayan's had indeed gotten it right. I mean, they were some of the first children of the earth that fought them off in the first invasion of this blue world but understand that these are not angels, and the son of man is not or was not among them. Too bad that the arrogances of man has his vision clouded. For it is going to take all that can be mustered by any known life form to date, just to correct this mistake brought on through arrogance.

But then and again, as it is, I am just here to observe the outcomes, then on to the next world. So when you really look at it, for me, it is only a report and a job somewhat. But for the whole of humankind, it is the life that no longer will be in existence if (in fact) they do not get it right this time, and by or through reading the writing which is upon the walls, literally.

"Why won't they ever get it right? Could they're whole existence have been disrupted or altered by our presents here?" These are just a few of the thoughts which run through my mind on any given day. For, I have seen this happen too many planets before, from the Alpha to the Delta Quadrant, and it is always the same. But for these people here, and because they refuse to heed the warning of the Mayans, Greeks, Egyptians, Romans, and the Children of the Stars who are my people, they shall soon be destroyed. For this story has played out many times over throughout the Universe, and always with the same results, destruction!

Look, even for a person like me, who really do like what it is that the Lord has put upon me to do. I still have a problem with the lack of change and towards a more proper form of evolution, which I have found in the many past humanoid species that now no longer exist. But how do I (as a humanoid examiner) explain to myself this thing which I can only call existence suicide and not feel some remorse for not intervening? *But then perhaps this whole thing was meant for me, and at the pleasure of The Lord who created everything, do you not think it so? Maybe this is something that I should consider as I go further with this piece.*

Moreover, maybe it is time for me to elevate to the next level of evolution for a lesser God, the elevated level of Creator. Thus, then he will allow me to create in his name, and byway of the *"Delta Quadrant,"* which is of *Hebrew Design*. But now, since you have been overlooking the advice of the past, I guess it might be your destiny that you follow the way of those many humanoid species of the past. Or who knows, it could well be my destiny to intervene this time and save the humans of this world.

Why? Because perhaps the time has come for them to be awakened and given a chance to break the cycle of the revolving door to destruction. Thus, maybe (I guess) the future of this world do lay in my hands (to some degree), one only knows!

But if I do this thing, then the only questions that come to my mind is: *"How will they indeed be able to evolve? I mean, if I do the work for them, then how will they learn who they really are from the inside out? For it is known that, for an entity to fully evolve to that next level of existence, that entity must first know thy self from the inside out fully.*

Thus, unlocking the secret of their real purpose, and for the pleasure of that, which has created us all from the beginning and until!" But with apologies, allow me to again refocus? For I have to consider the fact that it is not about me, but it is about you. And if on your own, you will be able to (for once) weather the storm or to advance and finally break the cycle of destruction. *"Will you ever attain your place among us, your siblings of creation, or will you find yourself like so many of the past. Simply a whisper upon the winds of the cosmos, an all cold and consuming part of the dark matter. A place known as time and space, liken to that of real estate seeking both to be discovered, as well as developed."*

I mean, though it pains deeply in the heart of me (that inability to intervene), this is what the job entails, and the assignment is what it is regardless of what I feel. For the thing I must feel first is to have faith in what it is that the Creator has asked of me to do, no questions asked. And if he asks of me that I destroy you, then that too I must do, no questions asked! For that is the greatest gift that we, as creations, can (in fact) give to a creator, along with having faith, loyalty, love, and respect, as well as remembering that we are but small cells that are a part of a grander and most Beautiful body, which happens to be the body of that who created us all, Our Creator!

But, if one who has wisdom really took the time, sat, and reread this from the beginning. Then perhaps he or she might be able to realize that, as much as I could not give you the secret. In simple words, it laid before you in all its glory, and all you have to do is find it okay?

~FOOT NOTE~

Since the ending of the year 2012, and on into the beginning of the end, many signs have been and will be revealed. But there comes a time when you have to wake up or change who you are and be who you were meant to be. If but for no other reason than curiosity, you must change. For the signs, tell us that you are running out of time. Okay, look! For you, it is your future to either live eternally or to be removed entirely.

But for me, it is a job; either way, be it you or some other form of creation, a report must be made, and that is my job writing and filling out reports for the Creator. Yet, in some small way, I feel that for me to be elevated to the next level of evolution, it is my duty to save you and by whatever means available to me. Thus, I choose the tool of the word. For it allows for one to both hear and have the option to read that which is quite essential, and for their advancement towards that most needed change. Or perhaps maybe it is arrogant and pride, which fuels this need to be considered by the Creator of us all, who is the Creator of Gods!

Either way, if it is the will that this thing I should do, then by me, it shall be done; thus, then it becomes destiny or meant to be. So I say to those with open ears seeking truth to be aware of the politics of man and to focus more on the love of his Creator. For in the deep darkness of your existence, that love flickers like a powerful beaming light to guide you back to him, 'Our Lord God Almighty, the true Deity.'

Look just take some time and think about it that is all I am saying. Because like I said before, for me, it is just a job either way. But what it is to you is something that you have to decide, like choosing either to continue down that same road or perhaps you will decide to go "Forward to Delta," and to a new beginning. Again thank you for your time, and as always, the hope is that something of importance you have received and that it will help you answer those questions of, "Are we alone among the stars?" and "Where do we go to from here?"

Kenneth Bernard Dean/LDD/Six (Author& Scribe)

CHAPTER 3

My Death My Life
One in the Same

~Author's Note~

Six days ago, I was confronted with (well how do I say this?), either a problem or another twisted blessing. I mean really when you consider who it is, we're talking about. Well this thing I guess we'll call it, took me to the edge if not to the front door of death. A place which I know much too well, a place I've been many times before. And for a moment, my thoughts were why knock just kick the damn door off the hinges, then face whatever I must to just get past it and move on to the next phase of this my journey.

But, then in the mist of going in and out of conscious, a voice like the one that comes each and every time I find myself in this kind of decision, spoke to me and asked me if I was up for a new adventure, one that is sure to prove to be promising? Well, when faced with a challenge like that without words, I agreed no questions asked. Thus, the journey toward my newfound knowledge about another part of life began.

A journey which further helped me, to understand how important life is, lack the selfishness, even though for most of my life, I felt it was about the training, and education for something more broader, and quite grander than just this life that I see around me in this "THE HERE AND NOW!

(LIVING LIFE WITH A DEATH SENTENCE)

I guess to start with, we must ask the question is it common to think about death or write about death, also why do people become uneasy when the conversation of death comes up? I mean are we that involved in the living aspect of life so much that we forgot the other side of the coin of existence, that being *DEATH!*

Is it not true that the purpose is that we were born to die, and from that we leave behind education for those left behind, things like how to be a part of life to the fullest, and how to die with dignity. Also, the individual's that make the transition of death will they all move into another form of reality. One that hopefully puts them that much more closely to the Lord the Deity, that which created us all.

Now as we get closer to that creative Deity, do we become more informed of where it is that this Deity comes from, and who created it, moreover do we become liken to him like Creative Deity's ourselves?

Thus, can we then say that we have evolved, and continue to evolve? I mean remember the paraphrases that are used in the great book of words, phrases like: *"The two sided sword, the meek that shall inherit the earth, the six verses the nine (which in a sense), becomes the ying and yang through a great deal of meditation, and a great deal of understanding; perhaps simply, it always speaks of left and right or the duality in life!"* I mean what does it all mean, does anyone know, can you explain?

Hence, the final reality is that you can't have one without the other so in true actuality, to go forward we (at some time), must all die or make that final journey to the other side where another reality awaits us.

Is it a reality slightly more evolved than the one that we just left, or do we become voices of the void of time and space, howling through the far reaches of time and darkness, like the chilling sounds of the wind blowing in a graveyard on a Halloween night?

Then and again there are those that will (in turn) through the knowledge, and education which they have acquired from the test of the trials and tribulations, within their own lives become what they have been prepared or created to be. That being Creators among the universe liken to that of what we call Gods or Deity's? And they in turn will create worlds, and on those worlds bring forth life upon them in many new designs and forms, thus feeding the need as well as the diversity of life, and also fulfilling the purpose of evolution and growth!

You know, often I see myself standing in the doorway of an ancient marble temple in my full nakedness, draped only by something similar to that of fine linen, standing among columns more grander than those of the Greek and Roman ruins of ancient times. Set among a hanging range of mountains which float among the heavens like emeralds cast there by some great hand of design and faith.

But in this hanging range of emerald wonders, I'm not alone. Even though I am content, the feeling there is the feeling of one who has transcended the need to be attached to those around me. Though the feeling of harmony still permeates the surroundings there, the connection or communication that I share with the others is purely spiritual among the inhabitants there.

Still I ask myself this question, *"Am I going crazy?"* But always the answer is the same and that is, *"What is crazy?"* Then I ask myself, "Is this normal?" and the question now becomes, *"What is normal?"*

"Is this how it is where I came from; is this the place where I consented to the call of the Creator to take on this great test of Trials and Tribulations?" Moreover, if this is so, upon the completion of this test will I be allowed to return to this place I call home?

Meanwhile, upon the completion of the test what do I leave to those of that latter reality, what important lesson that might inspire change toward positive forward movement? Is it a legacy of goodness, sort of like passing the torch to the next in line or will it be one of lost and unsettled despair, and if so, how much of the responsibility for that do I have to shoulder and for how long!

I wonder how many others among us have same or similar thoughts on these matters, and if so, are they many or are they few, and are they as dramatic and detailed in their thoughts. I mean, do they really think about it openly or is it just in passing by way of some euphoria or slight daydream. There are times when I look up into the heavenly sky and can almost feel the presents of something that is most powerful staring back at me.

Also, it gives me a sense of comfort, you know that feeling of being rapped up into the arms of some great and powerful protector, like that feeling of reassurance that an infant has in the arms of its parent.

Then almost like in an instance something touches me like real deep in my soul, and then I know that everything is okay. Thus, the thoughts of a dramatic leaving don't matter anymore, because when you think about it every leaving is a dramatic one. The only difference is if in fact, it was one of dignity or not.

Often, I think of leaving on a ship of reed and sail, like the ships that the Egyptians would place in the tombs of their great kings in route to that place where I so seek to be, that place where we evolve into Gods, that place I call home. You see I truly understand and know that there is another side to the coin of existence, but to me it is known to be the road back home or the road to the beginning thus the thought of death becomes a welcoming exit towards the journey home.

~FOOT NOTE~

We were born to die, and we die to be born again, this is the way to evolve to what lay ahead for the future of existence. For in this process we all will achieve what it is that await us in the end that being, to be liken to that of creators; "God like."

It is written in the book of words that "We and the Creator," are one in the same. But until we are complete, we will have to continue to transform ourselves to the level of God like perfection, which in a sense is the sum of the ability to be just, towards the ability to create on a mass scale universally.

Nonetheless, I can live knowing that both "My Death and My Life" are all One in the same! Again, thank you for your time and May the Almighty continue to shower you with his favors....

Kenneth Bernard Dean/LDD/SIX (Author and Scribe)

CHAPTER 4

Survivors' of the Wrath

~Authors Note~

As I sit here staring into a two-hundred-inch monitor, while traveling through the voids of time and space, at ten light-years short of light's speed. The reality of Earth's destruction once again comes to mind. Soon my mind is filled with an array of questions like, "What could we all have done, as a united humanity, to stop the destruction of our homeworld Earth?" "Or how could we have been so naive in thinking that our inherited dislike for diversity was more important than the salvation of our homeworld?" I mean, as we continued with our petty wars based on sheer ignorance, we allowed ourselves to be disillusioned. While all the time, we knew they were sitting just off the far side of our moon. Watching and waiting for just the right time to strike.

Though it is ten years pass since that day, it still feels like it was just last week when the first craft appeared and started to rain down destruction along the whole of the eastern seaboard, from the beachfront shores of Maine down to the Florida panhandle tip, and up to fifty miles inland. The destruction rained down, and anything within that area was (within a half-hour) no more.

I mean nothing or no one for a while could fight back or stand up to the overwhelming destruction, which came from those alien crafts from afar.

However, once we realized the sheer threat of complete annihilation, which was upon us. It became clear that for any to survive. We would have to put aside our childish bickering and work together to rid ourselves of this violation of humanity's right to exist. Unfortunately, though, millions survived, and we did manage to defeat them. We were still too late to save our world from its destruction. Thus, many left Earth for the new Earth colony, which came to be during those times. However, many like me thought it best for the settlement on the moon to survive. We would have to locate their world (through the use of their star charts) and end their lack of respect towards our right to exist.

Nonetheless, once again, I beckon you (the reader). To yet again, venture alongside me down a path as I journey into the realm of possibilities. Some positive, but most not so positive. However, keep in mind that though it may sound alarming, this "realm of possibilities" thing. One needs to understand, a "possibility" is a changeable thing when you give the opportunity of "change" a "chance!" So, without further ado, I give you the piece title "Survivors' of the Wrath," and like all my work prior. The real hope is that you both enjoy it while taking from it something to ponder later. Also, as always, I thank you for your readers' support.

SURVIVORS' OF THE WRATH

Chapter 1: Finally, the Day of Reckoning

"*During a meeting of the City Council, many items were before us to be reckoned for approval, by all there...*" The date is October 6, 2027, the time 0400 hrs., as we finally drop out of warp, revealing for the first time the Homeworld of our adversary. As expected, everyone on the bridge was at an all-time awe. For this world's view was not much different from the one we once knew, and call Earth our Homeworld.

It had large landmasses, similar to that of Earth of the past, surrounded by even more massive oceans of blue-green water, much like Earth as well. Moreover, the instruments at the bridge's environmental station show readings to be exact to Earth's environment and atmosphere. Had it not been for the fact this world was the size of our own Jupiter gas class world and had seven orbiting moons, it could have easily been mistaken for an Earth twin. However, the reason for our being here soon surfaced, and the order went out to the whole fleet to prepare for battle.

Soon we were given orders and directed to an area overlooking what appeared to be an industrial complex, surrounded by perhaps multiple military complexes. I was ordered once in place, to start the attack. So as we came on point, I gave the order to commence with the attack. Also, I gave the orders for drop troops to ready themselves for the land incursion leading up to the planned full-scale invasion of this world. I handed over command of the ship to my First Officer Jackson, for I felt it to be both my duty to go in with my troops and an opportunity for me to exact payback for all those lost and the lost world we all loved once. The world we once called Earth!

"Commander, this is your jump attack ship, and I'm your pilot, Captain Dickerson. If there is anything you would like to say to the troops at this time, please do it now, for we leave in ten minutes."

"Gather around troops. Well, as you all know, we are here for reasons forced upon us, and towards our survival. It is a known fact that some of us might not return alive, which is the sad byproduct of any war. However, remember that this sacrifice ensures that the next generation will have a chance to survive in a life of peace and prosperity. So, with that said, mount up, and let's give them hell!!"

Soon we were all tucked in and off heading toward our designated landing zones on the planet. The view from the window of the craft showed the sights of a tremendous ensuing battle occurring as I could see the destruction and debris of other troopships all around, while the pilot navigated over and through it all to get us to the landing zone. Many were praying as was me also, when the green light (signaling disembark) came on, followed by a loud voice repeating the word *"GO! GO! GO!"*

As I exited the craft, we were greeted by heavy fire from everywhere. As I watched troops dropping all around, the reality was one of real savagery. A savagery in pursuit of justice in the form of payback and for the attack ten years prior. An attack that took 1.5 billion lives and caused the destruction of our homeworld Earth.

"You men on the right, keep moving! Leave them, they are already dead! Keep moving the attack forward as ordered!!"

"Sir, the reports are coming in from all over this sector, and so far, the reports are all positive!"

"Thanks-First Sergeant!! Now connect me with the bridge of the ship, ASAP!!"

"Sir, I have the ship…"

"First-Officer Jackson, this is Commander Dean, prepare and drop the second wave for the mop-up of this area ASAP! Do you read, over!!"

"Commander, ETA for the second wave drop troops, is five minutes, over!!"

"Message received, over, and out!!"

"Lieutenant William, secure the area, and start loading the wounded to be shuttled to the medical ship ASAP!!"

"Sir, what about the prisoners, should I load them as well?"

"Not just yet! First load our wounded, then load our prisoners next, Okay!"

"Sir, yes sir!"

It is 0600 hrs., and for the moment, all seems quiet, though the war rages on in other areas of the planet. However, looking around, the view is that of sheer destruction. Moreover, the landscape (though alien), in some ways, reminds me of the rolling bluff filled mid-western states of America. Even though the inhabitants were quite different in appearance, to describe their appearance is to say that the mind of the Deity of creation is of an ongoing modification of design concepts beyond your wildest dreams.

But for the sake of simplicity, they shall be referred to as the Greens and the Grays of the Pleiades or best referred to as, the Seven Sister star systems. As my adrenalin level began to reduce itself, a sense of human emotions came over me. Especially when the alien survivors began to come out, from where they were hiding. Though they were aliens, the expressions on their faces and in their eyes spoke volumes in the form of fear. This fear was extremely prevalent in the emotional expressions and anxiety on the faces of their young. In many ways, this was quite unsettling for me, for I had experienced this ten years earlier, in the faces of our own young, on my planet Earth, when first they came.

Moreover, I wondered perhaps if maybe one, if any of the attackers of ten years ago. Could have felt the same when first they saw the faces of the many who had survived their first attack. However, this was no time for sentiments, for this was war, a fight for our survival in the Universe.

"Lieutenant William, are all the wounded loaded, and off-planet?"

"Yes Commander!"

"Okay! Then start loading the prisoners, starting with the young ones first. Remember, load them with the females and separate from the males, OKAY!!"

"As you ordered, sir!"

"Also, see if you can find me, someone, in a leadership position, to interrogate ASAP!"

"Affirmative, Sir!"

SURVIVORS' OF THE WRATH

Chapter 2: "Reflection"

"*Within minutes it was plain to see, these primitive people of the "Great Amazon River Valley" was in awe, as they pondered their reflections cast back to them within the mirrors, we so gifted them with...*"

It has been many years since we first invaded their Homeworld to retaliate for their attack ten years earlier against our Homeworld, *"Earth."* Yet, no one could have imagined the place in which both our people would find ourselves, and in these times. Moreover, though, the pain of the memories still hurt when the holiday VAAA Day or Victory Against Alien Aggression Day, comes up on the calendar. Both peoples of both planets manage to show compassion towards each other in the sense of unity, towards a brighter future for all our people. Today we see each other as allies towards a common idea. That being peace and prosperity, for both our people's generations well into the future and beyond. Yet, there are still threats out among the Universe's Stars, which appear threatening to both our peoples.

However, we have agreed to face these threats together, and for the good of both our people's. We have vowed never again to be enemies against each other. But to work together in exploring vast new ways of achieving those goals. For today is the birthday of an incredible vast pool of options to pull ideas from. To wit, we can all achieve those goals; thus, as I stand here looking out into the vastness of this, our newly found home, on this no longer alien world. It becomes clear that we are all in agreement with the task at hand. For, though we are foreign to this world in many or some ways, we are not. Because in a sense, who among you can say that perhaps, this was not the Lord's plan in the first place.

Anyway, right now, I have a taste for some Reticulin seafood and believe you and me, it is a most mouthwatering experience. For in many ways, it is better than the catfish I once use to indulge in from those greasy kitchens of any town back on old Earth. Well, it looks like the catch is in, so I have got to go. But understand one thing, if nothing else, it takes more energy to hate than it takes to show compassion. Thus, in the time I have left. I chose kindness and peace over everything else. So, in the words of the immortal Humphrey Bogart, *"Here's looking at you!"*

~FOOTNOTE~

Though this is just a story from "The Mind of Insanity." Things of this nature have been occurring since the dawn of man, and it continues to this day all across this planet Earth. For it is a known fact that we are a specie who thrive on the death and destruction of others to validate our own life. Perhaps soon, we might be able to correct this abnormal need within our specie, for death, blood, and sorrow. Because, though this may be just a story from "The Mind of Insanity."

The possibilities are still possible, providing we do nothing to change our state of being. As always, thank you for your time and interest. Also, I hope that you took from this something to ponder later. Again, thank you.

(Something to Ponder: From the Book of Six)
Kenneth Bernard Dean/LDD/Six (Author and Scribe)

CHAPTER 5

The Day Man Went Too Far

~A word from the Author~

This is one of those, "what if" concepts, and it raises questions of are we really ready to participate, and compete on a universal scale, with the rest of the worlds out there among the stars. So, just remember that it is only a "what if" kind of short story. One truly designed to make you (the reader) think, while enjoying the many different directions, the piece will carry you.

So, with no further ado, I give you the story "The Day Man Went Too Far" and as always. I hope that you at least, will enjoy it…

THE DAY MAN WENT TOO FAR

Chapter 1: The Dawn

Hi, my name is Don Dean'O. I am both the founder, and number one member of UNCLE. We're a planet born organization of people, who believe that through our faith in the Lords mercy, and by way of his grace. We shall, in keeping with the word, eternally live with the Lord. Yes, 'The United National Citizens League of Earth' (UNCLE).

Well as life would have it, again man would try his hand at tempting the Lord. Yes, again through his mismanagement of the gifts of science and technology, which the Lord had gifted upon them, along with the intervention of aliens, from a world abroad. He (man) has through his arrogant demeanor sold us out, and never saw it coming.

I mean, these creatures from afar had nothing but contempt, and hatred for our Lord and his children thereof. But there were people among us, who preferred the alliance with aliens saying: *"It can't be all that bad, and besides. With the incorporation of their specie, and technology within our world. Along with complete control over it all, our technology could advance by; how many years?"*

However, what they fail to realize was, they were truly out classed by these children of Lilith. Who happen (actually) to be the first wife of Adam. Moreover, the first human female Earth creation, of the Lord God, the Almighty.

I mean look, we're a world of many people, and we are the new kids on the block somewhat by planet standers. Plus, we were not so much out to make friends. As much as, we were out to steal their technology, from which the perfect A.I. could be, and was born.

Yes, a bio-mechanical life force, unlike nothing ever known to man. And to think, they could sale that idea to humanity, as a helpful additive to man-kinds evolutionary growth and future, was truly appalling.

But all the time, we were (meaning those in charge of our research, and development programs) sitting us all up (that being the whole of our world), for the takeover by, these Children of the Morning Star. Yes that, which sit at the left hand of our Lord the Deity, and who also was the first creation of the Lord before all things that followed. Thus, just as it was written. The members of the army of the Lord, this force called *"UNCLE."* Must now reveal to the children of this world. The true nature of this, the last war of Earths humanity. For the last book of the bible *"The Book of Revelation,"* is now set in motion. Thus, the survival of a people, as well as their home-world lay in the balance.

And to think: *"How ironic that only a few decades ago, we allow the leaders of this world, to separate the church and the state."* Thus, further creating this complete, and total split from that which created us all, Our Lord, the Almighty God. Furthermore, this intern gave them the power, to partake in this madness. But understand that because of this, for once man will soon be held accountable for their lack of faith, and bad judgment. Also, for the choices that was made on that day, in a time not so long ago.

Now, the whole of mankind, and throughout the world. Are sitting before flat screen televisions. Watching, and reaping the bitter fruits, of their bitter labor. Plus, realizing that there is nothing short of complete world destruction, which they can do to perhaps right the wrong. However, with nothing being done to stop it, at this point in our existence; is the one thing, which will make no difference anyway. For now, they truly realize the power over mankind, which they have given into the hands of the beast. For they are finally understanding truly, how deep the rabbit hole goes!!

THE DAY MAN WENT TOO FAR

Chapter 2: 12:00 Noon, and the Word is Out,

All Over the World

The sun was at noon day, and you could feel the panic in the air. Like a thick fog, it fell across the whole of earth. I mean, it was not like the people were out in the street type of panic, however a panic still! An eerie, and frighteningly kind of panic; like knowing that the last book of the bible is open. Why? Because you can see it openly on televisions, all over the world. Moreover, the feeling was that we as a world's people, can do not a dam thing to stop it.

Even at the headquarters, of the United States chapter of UNCLE. We along with the rest, watched this (our greatest sin, and man-kind greatest test), unfold before us on a flat screen, and there was that same eerie, frightening, panicky feeling. I guess knowing what we knew, gave us the rights above all else to feel that way.

I mean, the fact of having knowledge of what lay ahead for our world, and our people; I guess is why, the Lord our Deity prepared us. But who would've thought that it would arrive so soon. So now we, the children of the Lord the Deity, this UNCLE organization. Are all that stands between the loss of our world, and our way of life. Along with all the many ways, we practice our beliefs, and faith in the Lord along with our very existence!

But, if we fail! Then all that we are, our Lord, and Planet will either be under alien control or destroyed. So, knowing that (I guess), is enough to panic anyone. Plus, knowing that the safety of all that is, is hanging in the balance means someone has got to do the job. Well in my eyes that says, UNCLE!

"Okay! Everybody cut off those televisions and gather yourselves around please"... "Larry! Mitch! Pass out these papers, and make sure that everyone has one. Now please, move in closer!".... Now that was the voice of me, the so-called teacher, and leader of their clan. Larry, and Mitch well I call them my disciples, more so than my followers. Why? Because these two young men, I had become acquainted with them back in the day. For one night, when I was a member of that dark life style. Which was considered (at the time), to be a criminal life style.

I think, the Lord had a lot to do with me, and them taking to each other as well as we did. Sort of like they and I both, were in some way, given a second chance. Thus, I became their teacher, and they, my students, or disciples.

I can still remember how we came to be, and I can assure you. It was not one of those, *"hands shaking, how the hell are you!,"* type of acquaintance. Almost like yesterday, I can still see it clearly as if it were today. For it was late one evening, and I was in question over my beliefs, and had been for some time.

This was due to the fact, my whole family (my children, and their mother), was somehow lost to a car accident. I mean, I just could not phantom that the Lord, would allow that to happen. Moreover, at a time in my life, when I was finally free from the despairs, of those hardships. Which had for so long, pillaged me throughout the whole of my life.

It was like all the hurt, and pain somehow build itself up in me. I was to the point of just wanting to be with them, and by any means available. So, being of a clouded mind. I took off that night, to get high on drugs and alcohol. You know just to relieve the pain, and loneliness that at the time, occupied my heart.

I was in one of the worst places in the city, the North side. I mean, for a police officer to find five or six dead bodies a night was nothing. Plus, from the looks of the two-people heading my way (both Larry, and Mitch) that perhaps, I myself might be a candidate for either, slot five or slot six. You know, depending on how many John Doe's there were already that night. The only comfort I had, was under the influence of the drugs, and alcohol; being killed by these two, might just be a painless venture to final peace for me.

"So, to hell with it, and just do what it does," was the comforting statement that came forward that night. As I hooded up. I thanked the Lord and headed toward what I thought was my ending destiny. But, to no avail. For suddenly, a feeling came over me. No pain, just a feeling, and one I couldn't begin to describe.

All I remember is, waking up three days later. In the presents of these two guys, Larry, and Mitch as they began to tell me, they were not there to rob or to bring harm to me. But that they, themselves, were sent to me by the Lord to assist me in any capacity I saw fit, less death. Now hearing this, was like a most needed comfort. Like the kind one requires, after a long journey to nowhere and back.

However, both Larry and Mitch in a sense, I believe were angels. Sent by the Lord himself, to comfort me in this my time of great need through the pain I so suffered. But later I would grow to understand, the true reason for their being along with, the Lords true purpose for my existence.

I can still remember the feeling; I would get whenever they referred to me as teacher. Like something or someone more than just me. They would (though I refused to believe it), tell me that I would be in someways, responsible for the salvation of humanity here on Earth. Also, I was the key to teaching them, what it's like to be human. All the while, believing only on this anchor of faith alone; just to get me or whoever through it, in this day to day existence. Also, there was that other feeling, which only I would get. The one where you feel that the Lord himself, was talking to you, and teaching you things. You know, the kind of things that would be most needed soon, if we are ever to survive this threat to our existence from afar. However, this was a time of war or a situation seven years in coming. Plus, only a few world leaders, had any knowledge that this world and its alien beings, even existed.

Thus, this was the start of a seven-year ministry. One that would take me all over the world, from port town to big city. Preaching the word and giving love to those that needed it. Why? Because they were the ones, who the world governments had decided, were not worthy of life.

Plus, they were set to be replaced, by this new entity, known to us only as *"Artificial Intelligent"* or *"AI."* But, through my teaching of the word. They or many of them, could hold on to their hopes, their beliefs, and to fight for what was important to them, which in fact is their lives. They also began to trust again that they, would be protected by the word of the Lord. For, now they were becoming again, one with the Lord the Deity.

THE DAY MAN WENT TOO FAR

Chapter 3: "The Preparation, for what is to Come"

"*Can you believe it, they went ahead and did it,*" … "*They opened the way to our own destruction, a door better left closed*" … "*Okay! Everybody, lets pay attention!*" … "*Now the events of the day, we all knew were to be. I mean, I know that some of you are worried about the future. But understand people, we above all the others must keep our heads, if we as a people have any chance at all!*" … "*All those days spent combing through the Book of Revelations, trying to find the key, to turning this mess around just might pay off.*" … "*But remember we have got to stick together, for the strength of our salvation, lies in our unity and combined faith. So, let's pull together, and remember your teachings, Okay?*" …

As I spoke to my clan, I told them that this was not the time to run and hide in fear. But the time for UNCLE to finally stand up and take back our world. Understand for me this was a God sent. An opportunity to really do some good, not just for friends and family. But, for people all over the world. Also, an opportunity, to finally use the training that the Lord, had passed down to me and it felt good!

"*But how do we stop these transgressions, which stand before us and our faith? … Like, how do we teacher?*" … "*Look, I can't say that it's going to be easy or even that I have a master plan. You know, one that I can just pull right out of a pocket now. But what I can say, is that it's not too late, to try everything we've been studying for the last seven years."*... *"I mean look, first things first, and what we have to do is pull our people back to a safe place. So, on that note, I say we should get started!"* ...

As I was talking to the people in my clan, once again this great feeling came over me. It was like the feeling of knowledge had been thrust upon me, like that of a thick covering of pressure. But it was neither stressing or of a burdensome. It was a feeling that allowed me, to accept who I was, and who I am now. Then it came to me, for the Lord do know the whole of us, inside and out. You know, this new and good me. As well as that me, which we best not talk about or even remember.

So, if our past doesn't matter to the Lord once we have given our lives over to him. Then giving your life up for him should be a blessing, and not a worry don't you think?

Now later that evening before we left for the new base camp, it must have been about six o'clock. Like just before the sun prepared to go down, making way for the night. When we all decided, the best way to start the journey was first with prayer. So, on bended knees, we all pledged to give our lives up, for our beliefs and our world. Thus, reassuring that the will to live, was one tide to the word.

Also, too fight against, the evilness of those men, and their alien alliance with the children of Lucifer. Moreover, the time for hiding out in dark places, to preach the word to the Lords children is over! For it is time, for an all-out assault against the enemies of the Lord, and the lost children of this planet as well! Now, we may not know, how we're going to defeat, these bio-mechanical soldiers yet.

But what we do know is, they were built by the hands of man, and the technology is that of their alien friends. Then someone in the group asked. Against that kind of technology, what can we do? Now this is one of those worrying thoughts, which I know crossed my mind, and perhaps all present in the clan that day.

Then it came to me, as I started with: *"Well let's just look closer at this. For if the Lord created us, and in his own image and design. Then we as children, trying to copy this same concept idea of creative design. Would probably incorporate, some of those same human abilities, and flaws in those copies or artificial intelligent beings as well."* ... *"I mean, this has always been the desire of evil men. That being, to create life either by cloning or through the mechanical building of them, and by way of the technology for bio-mechanical beings."*

"However, man is quite fragile. Both mentally, as well as physically. Plus, anything that he builds, will have those traits, and flaws implemented in the design as well. I also feel, we can count on the fact that man, will give a heart and a brain to this abomination. Thus, if so, them that is where we will find its weakness!" ... "So, what you're saying, is that a shot to the heart or brain region, will kill it or them?" ...

"Yes and no!" ... "Okay, understand what we have here, is a new life form. The birth of a new conscious; yet a spiritually unaware being. One that can learn, using a heart and brain. Also, it may suffer the flaws, of the weakness of emotions, and those just might be our best or only weapons." ... "Just look at the possibilities, if we can change just one of them, and then release him back with a message of change built into those emotions. Perhaps, he might be able to do the work for us by influencing more of them, sort of like the domino effect!" ... "So, what you're thinking is that we can convert them, right?" ... "Yes!" ... "Oh, come on, next you'll be saying that they'll be in heaven with us!" ...

"Okay look people, I know that it sounds crazy. But don't we teach that the body, is just a vehicle that the soul uses to travel around through life in." ... "Is it not true that this soul, is nothing more than energy. A life force, which one day will be lifted up into the heavens, to live eternally with the Lord the Deity?" ... "Look, I am only saying try, and see the broader picture here. That being, the soul as either negative or positive life energy, while the body as a vehicle which that energy occupies and utilize for traveling. Much like our own situation. Now whether the vehicle is born of the body of man or of man's factories should matter not." ...

"For the purity of the energy, which is the soul. Is all that matters here, and there is purity there. Thus, I say to you, they can be converted, and convert them we shall!!"

THE DAY MAN WENT TOO FAR

Chapter 4: Encounter with

The New Life Force

Now, the morning of the next day is finally here. However, it seems to be unlike previous mornings, and rightly so. For it was the first day that man, and machine would come face to face with each other. Moreover, this was also the day that man, and his alien friends had planned to unfold their plans of a perfect *"one world order."* Along with this new race of *"artificially intelligent beings"* upon us all. Yet the feeling in the air, was one of unrest and deception. Nonetheless, my people and I, were not going to have it or even go out like that!!

"Hurry up, hurry I say! We must get our people out of the city, as soon as possible!" ... *"Everything must be moved to the mountains, for from the caves we came, and to the caves we shall return, now hurry please!"*

Now, I was just about to light up my last cigarette, when then it happened. First the sky looked like it was on fire, then with sounds of thunder it seemed to open, and out of it came the first crafts of the alien visitors.

I could only look with amazement, for the next thought that came to mind, was the Book of Ezekiel. Where in it, he (Ezekiel), speaks of a wheel of fire, spinning with in another spinning wheel of fire. As the first craft came closer, like in the Book of Ezekiel.

Creatures did in fact come out of this mighty craft and hurled themselves towards the planet. Now, as this was happening in the distance, I could see more of these big crafts. Like large platters hanging in the sky, were the view that fell upon my eyes that early morning. As astonished as I was to see it, it was soon disrupted by the shouts of Larry.... *"Please teacher, the trucks are loaded, and we must leave!" ... "We have to go now, for we must make it to the mountains before night fall!"* ...

Now, like in a flash I was back, and focused, for Larry's plead had did its job. For he was one that worried about everything, mostly me. And I can only describe him, as one that both loved the Lord whole heartedly, and I believe he would even die for me (if it ever came to it), just to keep the work of the Lord in full swing. For to him, he was doing the work of the Lord. Thus, in many ways, to die for a person who is doing the Lords work, is to die for the Lord himself.

Nonetheless, as I was walking towards the trucks. I can still remember looking up into the sky and thinking about the task that lay ahead. I mean, it finally came to me in all its true glory. That being, my true purpose. For the real battle was yet to be fought, and by this little ragtag army that now was crammed into these trucks and heading out of the city for the mountains. As I was climbing into the truck and preparing my mind for the new life and task ahead. I looked towards the horizon and could see about four or five more formations with about fifty crafts in each coming from the east, and equally the same coming from the west.

"Is everything secured?" ... I asked... *"Make sure the two-way phones are working and let everyone know that we're taking the back roads out Okay!!"* ... *"But teacher, now that the people are in panic mode, wont the back roads be jammed up as well?"* ... *"Look, that's why I need everyone, to stay close together on the back roads. Also, let them know that once we come to the river road, we'll be going south so stick together, and keep those two-way phones open, Okay? Actually, you better give me the phone!"* ...

"Pay attention people, we're going to take the back roads east for two miles, till we come upon the river road. Where we will turn south towards the mountains, keep in mind that we must reach the caves before

nightfall!" ... *"Understand people! By tonight, government troops along with state troopers and local police officers, are going to close down all the exits leading out of the cities."* ... *"Already all major road ways; like the highways in and out of the cities, have been closed. Plus, they will be looking for headlights throughout the night, so keep it close and we'll be fine, Okay?"*

Even though we were in flight, out of the city. We all knew that come morning, anyone left in the city would need an act of God to leave. Also, the longer they were there, the harder it was going to be to get even that.

By twelve midnight, we were pulling into the mountain compound. Soon after we began to unload the trucks, when over the compound speakers, a bulletin was being broad-casted to the area. It informed us that there was a curfew in effect inside and up to five miles outside the cities of the world, in all directions. Anyone found moving around in those areas after curfew, would be arrested, locked up, and held for questioning. I think they said it had something to do, with the alien alliance safety measures. Drawn up in the *"technological treaty for unity plan,"* which they signed with the visitors twelve years earlier.

"Teacher! teacher! come quick! We have Asia on-line, with a situation report. We are about to start downloading the message now, so you need to be there for the reading of it!" ... As I turned to my right, I could see that it was Mitch who was talking ... *"Thanks Mitch, again you've done well in your choice of locations. Have someone show Larry, and the others were to store the food, water, and medical supplies. Then join me, in the communication bunker. Also bring Dr. James, and Sister Lilly back with you, okay?"* ...

Now, Dr. James was a rather slim sort of a man. Plus, he was well versed, in both the field of medicine, as well as biotechnology. For me, I was glad that one so versed in these two fields of science, was now embarking with that same enthusiasm towards his faith. I pray every day for this brother, for his task shall become greater than he can ever imagine: *"Oh Lord Deity, bless this brother for in the coming days, he shall truly be tested!"* is the words that I would use when, I prayed for this brother. Then there was Lilly, sister Lilly, is what we all called her. I really don't know how or why she came to be called that. However, what I do know is that from the start, it's been that way maybe because it fits.

Then again, maybe it's because of the way she takes care of us all. Like that of a younger sister, who has much love for her older brothers and sisters. Perhaps that is the reason why her job interest, is the monitoring of the food, water, and medical supplies. As well as assisting the good Dr. James medically whenever. I must say, if there were ever a person's presents that was ever closed to being called angelic, and a blessing it would have to be hers. Finally, we come to Mitch. One of those malty extra-ordinary personalities, governed by the love that he has for both the Lord the Almighty God, and all that this great and most benevolent creator has created, and one who I will talk more about later.

Now from the communication bunker, I again heard someone call out to me…. *"Teacher! teacher come quickly! the message is complete, and ready for your decoding, Hurry!"* …Now that was the voice of Rick, the young brother, which Mitch put in charge of both the communications, and the communications bunker… *"Okay! I'm on my way!"* … As I went into the bunker, I could hear the voices of both the good Dr. James, and Sister Lilly… *"Wait up, before closing that door teacher"* … *"Hurry then, for there is much that must be done. Already a message from our contacts in Asia has been received, and it requires my decoding skills. So, we might know a little more, about the world outside. Plus, I need both of you there as well, so hurry up!"*

As we three rushed into the bunker, and down the stairs; we were soon confronted by a somewhat, chunky kid with light blond hair. His hand was extended out, with the message held firmly in it…. *"Here! right here teacher! this is the message from Asia. Plus, the one from the Euro-Congress, is coming through over the wires as we speak!"* … *"Rick is it, or should I call you Ricky?"* … *"It doesn't really matter sir, that's up to you."* … *"Then I've always been fond of Rick, so Rick it is."* …Those were the words that were spoken, as I took the message from his hand, and prepared to decode it…. *"Take your time son, the world is not going to leave us yet, at least I hope not."* … *"Contact Mitch and have him come to the communication bunker's conference room, for the briefing. Also send the message from the Euro-Congress along with him when you finish receiving it, all right?"* … *"Sure sir!"*

As I started to decode the message, I was not at all stunned by the report that their country also was under invasion by these alien friends. However, the thought of the Euro-Congress message saying the same thing, was not going to be much of a surprise either. Soon shortly thereafter, there was a knock at the door, to the conference room...

"Enter!"... "Well, I thought that it might be you, come on in and take a seat!... Rick from communications, went to receive the Euro-Congress message, and he will be sending it with Mitch because I want him here at this briefing as well."... "Now, I would like to take the opportunity to introduce you, to the rest of the people here in my group while, we wait for Mitch to get here, with the message from the Euro-Congress."

"To the left is our good Dr. James, who oversees the hospital, and all medical problems that might surface in these times. Also, he heads our bio-technology team... Next to him is the good Sister Lilly, who is responsible for monitoring our food, water, and medical supplies. ...Plus, she assists Dr. James, whenever and wherever needed... Dr. James and Sister Lilly, this is General Parker. He was sent to us, by our friends in Washington some six months ago, when they found out about this plan."

"For a while, we had to suppress the knowledge, of our friend the good General... So as not to compromise him or his ability to use his position to move in and around, the workings of Capitol Hill, the Pentagon, and the White House... Now with that out the way, I'll hand the meeting over to the General"...

"First, let me thank you all for being here, and allowing me time that you don't have, to bring you up to parr on our present situation... Make no mistake we are under attack by alien forces, and with the help of our own leaders... Whether knowingly or unknowingly, the fact remains... That being that we are under attack, and by outsiders of our solar system!"... "Also, what we realize, is that our leaders seem to be powerless towards these aliens, and are truly unaware of the massiveness of this problem...

"I have had communications, with my overseas counterparts throughout the world. However, the reports received is that this problem is the same with leadership, in their countries as well! It's like these alien creatures seems to have powers, far greater than what we're used to dealing with! I mean, powers that we've never imagine ever could exist

in a living organism… It's like the whole world, is becoming victimized into slavery, and by this mind controlling special ability of theirs."

"In fact, as we sit here. I can truthfully say that our planet, the one that existed yesterday, is no more. And I know that we have been subjected to an attack or should I say an invasion, by these so-called friends of man along with their so-called, bio-mechanical gift to humanity!"

"I mean, just look around; for these creatures from outer space, seems to be spreading out over the face of this planet, like a pestilent." … "At last report, from forward positions throughout the world… They have not yet become aggressive… "However, at their rate of growth, real soon their numbers will be greater than ours… Thus, if or when they decide to become aggressive or violent, well need I say more!" … "Now on the other hand, what we do know is that their whole agenda is or seem to be, conquest by way of mind control… This means they can attack us in our dreams, so even in our sleep we're not safe… Thus, from the materials, and information that we have gathered… We know that we have a real problem on our hands, and it's only going to get worst as time goes on, thank you!"…

"I thank you for that briefing General, and now we will open the floor to our own Dr. James, in the hope that he might be able to give a more scientific over view of the situation, so doctor if you please?" …

"Thank you Don Dean'O, and General Parker. First, I can say that there might be a slight chance we may be able, to put up some resistance against these abominations."

"But we must act as soon as possible, this means we must get to one of those bio-mechanical beings and bring it here for research and study at the soonest! … But the question is, how to do this without compromising our safety, as well as the safety of this hidden community!" …

"Okay! again thank you doctor, and if there is nothing else, then I will ask now; that we should consider, all possible avenues of approach in this matter. So as not to put at risk, the safety of our mission as well as our faith, and our planet… So, with that in mind, let's get started, OK?" …

Now, with that everyone got up. But, before they could go any further. I turned and reminded them that what they had heard here in this bunker, was to stay here until further notice. Then they went out of the room… *"Ah, General, can I have a word with you before you* leave?" ... "*Sure, this way please!*" ...Suddenly, and before we could even get started, Mitch came in with the message from the Euro-Congress hot off the wire... "*I'm sorry for not being at the briefing, but once you read this, you'll understand why.*"

As he handed the message to me, I could see that whatever it was it had him frightened, and that brought fear upon me... "*Thank you, but maybe you should have a seat.*"...That's what I said as I took from his hand this folded piece of paper, and began to read what was written on it...

"*General! You've got to see this; it seems that the worst came a lot sooner than projected... It looks as though the Euro-Congress has in fact declared a state of war between the alien, and their human allies as we speak... Plus, they are asking that the rest of the world's forces, do the same!*" .... "*NO!... HELL NO!!*"... "*GOD-DAM-it!!*"... It can't be true... You must have decoded the message wrong; I mean this cannot be true*" ... "*They must all be mad; we cannot hold out against their kind of technology along with their mind control abilities... I mean, at the least this is nothing less than a blood bath!*" ...At that time, someone knocked on the door very loudly... "*Come in!*" ...Then as the door opened, I could hear the news reports over the voices of the people in the outer room. The reporters were giving a blow by blow report of the ongoing battles.... "*My god, there goes another explosion, bodies are being thrown every which way!*" .... "*Men, women, and children are being tossed around like so many leaves to the wind... Moreover, it seems to be no end in sight to this kind of destruction, and devastation that is being handed out by these aliens, and their weapons of mass destructions!*"....

Then as quickly as the report came, it went. The whole channel went silent as if it never were. As my eyes surveyed the faces in the room, it kind of reminded me of some kind of really bad B-movie, you know the ones with heroes. But, we all knew, this was no movie of kind. For we all knew that this was real as hell and was soon to get a lot worst.

Plus, we knew also, the idea of a hero coming to the rescue was just that; an idea or if you prefer, a distant dream. For there was not going to be any heroes coming, less it be us ourselves who are the true heroes!

"I must get back to Washington D.C., and it can't wait!" … *"Don Dean'O, you and your people, better hope that your Lord can hear your prayers. Because we are going to need all the support that he can give us if we're ever to survive this war!"* … *"All I can say to you all at this point, is do all that you can to hold out. But, if worst comes to worst get out as fast as you can. I'll try to keep in contact as well as get you more supplies. But know this, at this point right now, there are no guarantees!!"* … And with that he, the General, left in a haste!

~FOOTNOTE~

When you look at all that man has evolved into, and the great accomplishments they have made. It makes you wonder truly about, the future of us all, and that is frightening. Moreover, for them to have that kind of power in a sense, has proven to be pretty much the conundrum. Yet in their hearts, they have still not changed enough to even make a difference. However, at this late stage in the game. The question of: "Really, why should it matter?" is something that you all should look at and ask questions about.

Also, to think that someday soon, the visitors of other worlds will soon be at the door steps of this, your world. Is not that far fetch or hard to conceive. For in the many lives, which I have been privy to have lived. It is a fact that it always starts out the same, each and every time.

Thus, the question then becomes: "Are we truly ready or are you truly ready for what's heading fast this way? Or perhaps what is it that you can or must do, to prepare yourselves in protection, for this great coming? Nonetheless, the true question at the end of the day still becomes, "What Do We Do?"

(Eighth Law: From the Book of Six)
Kenneth Bernard Dean/ LDD /SIX (Author and Scribe)

CHAPTER 6

The Elephant in the Room

~A Word from the Author~

"How often is it that you find yourself lost when it comes to understanding reality?" "Or worried if what comes out of your mouth is a thing truly understood as your view of a situation or event through your eyes. Yet, still, a thing which is open for discussion towards a more acceptable solution, as opposed to violence?" "Or maybe you have problems finding the right words to address an individual ethnicity or race of people, and feel that if a mistake is made there in the start of the conversation (by misidentifying the said group of people); it may prove to be more harmful, than if you had never opened your mouth in the first place seeking to right the wrongs?" It is a proven fact that when you place "racial diversity" as an ingredient of politics, then what you are really doing is building an "ill social ideology or simply a society of chaos" controlled by the tool of conflict.

Yes, something as simple as basically the right word or words to adequately address an individual's race or ethnicity is the one thing that is keeping everyone away from the table. And it does not matter if the table is square, round, or triangle-shaped, the fact is: "There is no one sitting at the table, regardless of what the shape of the table is!" Now, when no one is sitting at the table and talking about the problems. Then, the only thing that happens is the problem mature into this even more significant problem and so on.

Now, soon after this effect began, you will see a multitude of social issues occur; things like racial tension, poverty, a decline in education throughout society, a growth in crime, which are hate crimes perpetrated racially, or even gender specific.

A society where the institutions sit up to serve and protect the citizens, resort to our youth's mass killings, and on a scale equal to that of America's Pre-Civil War and Reconstruction years. Sort of like, they have replaced the good old slogan of "Serve and Protect" to this brand-new slogan of "To Kill and Collect"!! Pretty much like back in the earlier mob days when the CIA, the FBI, and the Justice Department played footsy with the Five Families. However, this is a lot more Political, and a whole lot deadlier for the youth of all ethnicities. Though maybe not so much now, however, nonetheless, this is the actual plan. That being too, through acts of deception, manipulate the thinning of the herd, and to a point or level that is both acceptable along with being not so much of a problem to control.

Of course, when something genuinely vile occurs, like most things these days. Then for a moment, it becomes big news. The kind of story that sells papers, books, magazines, and gain broadcast ratings for the news networks. But in the end, it does nothing to address or cure the problems at hand. However, whenever those problems do occur and somehow do bring forth the gathering of a diverse group of people into a Room or Hall to start the discussion. There always seems to be this "uneasiness" within the atmosphere. This "uncommon ground" feeling among many of the participants, leading them to think or feel a sense of irrelevancy.

This thing I am talking about is a syndrome and one that we all need to get beyond soon if ever we are to survive, as well as conquer these social ills. Yes, this thing I am speaking of is "commonly" known as "The Elephant in the Room" syndrome. Though unseen, it is still powerfully tangible, and it has stopped the forward movement of the "American Society" for far too long.

This Elephant, which has caused the people of this Country much grief, heartache, pain, division, and misery for far too long, is truly the one issue we cannot afford to let take president over the big picture. Thus, like a hunter with a big gun, we must (with words) shoot down this proverbial "Elephant in the Room."

Thus, this is the nature of this piece, "The Elephant in the Room." A short piece dedicated to doing just that, removing this (though unseen, still tangible) beast from among us. This beast that we (ourselves) designed to destroy the fiber of this social structure of humanity, and the culture thereof as well.

So, with no further ado, I give you "The Elephant in the Room." Also, like always, the hope is that you both enjoy and take something of importance to ponder later and in the hopes of coming up with a solution.

TOWN HALL MEETING

Within the auditorium, at which point the "Town Hall Meeting" was to be held. There was a sense of uneasiness, which filled the air as many there, separated themselves into ethnically specific groups, not all but some. However, as I moved among them, hoping to get a feel for the crowd's mood. I was shocked at some of what I heard coming from those specific groups.

Things like:

"Well, when we address them, what is the proper title?"

"For the one thing we do not want to do is to start this discussion offending anyone or any group. So, with that being said, does anyone have any suggestions?"

Now upon hearing this, I became more saddened than angered by what I had heard. For at that moment, I knew that because of the beast, which encompassed the group there like a standing cloud among them, there could or would be no solution to any of the problems set for discussion. Moreover, it was plain to sense that indeed "The Elephant in the Room" had won once again...

It is a known fact that we humans consider ourselves to be a highly intelligent species. The smartest of all the species on this planet Earth. I mean from Man, came all the wonders of modern ideas. Things like current technological concepts and machinery, which help to make life possible over a vast amount of the surface of this planet Earth.

We have also (to some degree) conquered vast milestones in medicine and human health practices extending life in many ways. We are also capable of overcoming extensive engineering projects and or programs. Our curiosity over our sense of place in the

Universe has opened the door to new scientific explorations far beyond this small rocky World we know to be called Earth.

Every day we are discovering new places light-years from us and anticipating one day to stand on the shores of a vast body of water on those places or to climb to the top of a great Mountain peak within a great range of Mountains, on a World thousands of light-years away. All this and much, much more we are capable of, for this is our created right, handed down by the creator to us all. Yet, when you actually look at us, the one thing that truly stands out. Is that we are viewed as a specie moving around our planet surface, with our heads up our asses. I guess that is why dogs see us like their own shit picker-uppers.

We (perhaps to our knowledge) could probably be the only World of complete diversity to exist. Not to say that there may not be other Worlds where life does exist within the Universe. But to date, all we know of is Earth, which is so crucial at this point right now. Yet, though, we are the accomplisher of these and so many more incredible accomplishments. There is still that elusive dark side within us all, and our World's social structure, which destroys the purity of this God created human concept. A thing which taints our past, presence, and now it is threatening the future fiber of the existence of us all.

For it is a darkness, which is in-breaded deep into the DNA of humanity the World over. This thing, which drives an unimaginable hate towards the beauty of a most diverse and beautiful idea of creative genius. An Idea, and one we all should feel blessed to be a part of.

However, we see this beautiful diversity as a way to grasp power through the introduction of chaos and conflict. For the force spilling of blood, in a senseless act towards the domination, control, and strength over others are what is birth from such a vile relationship.

"Moreover, (in a sense) somebody opened the doors, and let a herd of elephants lose, and running wild throughout the mindset of humanity the world over." In fact, the powers to be are so good at this form of control (that) they use it to control the World Economy, along with the rise and decline of the human population as well.

So, when you really take the time and really look closely at it all; you began to understand (entirely) the need for war, poverty, racial tension, low self-esteem, crime, addictions of all kinds (drugs, alcohol, etc.), and of course this self-hate for humanity within some if not all of humanity.

Yet, something as simple as how to address a person of a different ethnicity, with a descriptive word of pride and dignity, should be the least of our problem. For, to deal with just that problem alone is relatively easy, especially when you see the person as both equal and human. Rather than just finding dis-stain in the hue of the ethnicity, skin color, and or cultural gifts of the said person or group.

We all need to accept that there is a purpose for it, you know, the whole ethnicity, skin color, and or cultural gift thing, and that purpose is the beauty of diverse creativity.

However, as I close this piece, I still cannot help thinking that of the many who might get the opportunity to read what I have written. Only a few will even get the jest of what it is they have read, and still, some will take it as a mind wondering manifesto of hate or blame. Nonetheless, somewhere deep down inside, perhaps you will begin to feel or believe as I do with a little more time. Moreover, who knows, maybe that might be the best thing (in a long time) to happen for or to you.

So, with that being said, I thank you all for your time. Also, like always, I hope that you both enjoyed it, as well as took from it something to ponder later. Till next time, please keep an open mind. Bye!

~FOOTNOTE~

The last time I ever filled out an employment application, something came over me when it got to the form's racial question. At which point you give your ethnicity, and by way of choosing either the proverbial labeled race box with an "X" or by circling the big, bold first letter of the nationality or race of your belonging. However, I, in turn, tried something different.

For I remembered a time in my youth, when my Grandmother, after being questioned by me as to what race or group I belonged to and my skin color. At that time, she (my Grandmother) told me to bring the 64-count box of Crayola crayons. After which she informed me many years ago, I was not black. But a most beautiful, slightly dark sierra brown, I never forgot that. For that was indeed the first time I ever felt equal and with purpose as a part of God's human creation.

Thus, as I looked further down in the area of that question, I was able to locate the box labeled "OTHER" and proceed to fill in the space, with what my Grandmother had both told and showed me on that day. That being, "A Slightly Dark Sierra Brown, North American Born, Representative of Earth." Needless to say, I did not get the job.

But upon leaving, somehow, whether or not I got the job was not an issue. But the one important thing is the pride I felt for myself and the ability of the Lord to create in such a vast array of diversity. However, that personal concept was fulfilling enough. So, to Grandma, thank you for that simple yet powerful talk. For it opened my eyes to who and what indeed everyone, as well as myself, is.

That being, a color from a 7.2 billion count box, of the Lord God's own Crayola crayons in a sense; so, to those who have a problem using "Black or White" to explain your ethnicity, do the simple thing, and go buy a box of 64 counts Crayola crayons.

Now, if (by chance) that do not work for you, take it back and ask for the 128-count box, for I am sure you are in there somewhere amongst the many beautiful hues. "Oh, Snap!" got to run; it seems as though someone let an Elephant into the room again. So, it looks like I will be busy with getting rid of yet another "Elephant in the Room" again; later!!

Kenneth Bernard Dean/LDD/Six (Author)

CHAPTER 7

The Paradox of the Empathetic Entity

~Author's Acknowledgement~

*T*he fact of the matter is, we as simple human beings, find it quite hard to accept the responsibility of our actions wholeheartedly. But at the same time, we want all that life has to offer, without even considering that in the end there are still those consequences. Yet to be owed, by either the HOLDER of that unpaid debt or the EMPATHETIC ENTITY, which we so call our LORD.

Through this short concept, I hope to at least implant a sense of open mindedness or maybe inspire curiosity in the reader of this piece. Remember OPEN MINDEDNESS and CURIOSITY breeds HOPE...

In the beginning, there was just time, and space throughout the darkness of the void, and this was a good thing. Then there was the voice, and the voice called me by name. Thus, I came to be, and this also was a good thing. Now for a long time, I was content with just the voice and myself. Now, there came to pass a time. When the voice came, and thought that I was alone, and with too much time on hand with no one or nothing to share it with.

So, this great, and most powerful voice brought forth light and revealed his self to me. Now, when I saw this great creator of worlds, and life for the first time. I was compelled to drop down before him (this great light), on bended knees in the dark comfort of the void, and praised him for showing the wonders of his self to me!

Then I heard the voice of creation, and it said, *"I am the great I AM,' that, which is the creator of both life and worlds. The Alpha and the Omega, for when I spoke, a vast universe came to be."*

As I listened, with one mighty voice from this God of creation (and before me) a vast collection of universes came to be and was laid out before me. For as far as I could see, and in the darken voids of time and space they continued to expand out. Like gem stones on a carpet of black velvet, were these newly created universes. Moreover, like a fist of sand thrust before the winds of time, they were likening to, as they came to be from just his word alone. Thus, I knew then that he was (in fact) the true Lord, the Deity that most High of the Highest, my Father!

Now, though I should have been overjoyed by this great and well thought out gift, to end what was considered to be my loneliness. The only thing that I felt, was anxiety. For it was then clear to me that perhaps, I (in some way) was not to the design expectations, of this "The Most High." I mean, like a fever it was embedded in my soul. This knowledge of my Lord, and Father no longer to be known as mine and mine alone. For through his spoken words, this was to be no more. Why, because that creation that came from those words (like an invasion), took that away from me, and this saddened me very much.

"Why are you so sad?," was the next thing that I heard, *"Does this not please you?"* followed soon after. Now for a moment, all I could do was just stare. You know, like a mystifying stare from the deep darkness, of time and space itself. I mean, just looking at all that wonder stretching out before me, should have helped me to give some suitable thanks of gratitude for such a gift. *"But no, I was not happy nor pleased with the fact that now I should share our time with all that you've now created,"* was truly the thought which kept running through both my heart and mind. *"What have I done to warrant such a displacement of our time alone?"* was what I felt and asked.

Now for a moment, the mood seemed to be of an uneasiness, but somewhat comforting. Then like the sounds of rolling hooves, of a mighty herd of large rushing animals came the sound of this, the mighty voice of the "Great I Am," he who is the creator of all things great and small. Like complete universes of time and space, ever building in both my ears, and my mind. Thus, I found myself once again, felled before this great light, of designed wonder. This my Lord, my Deity.

Why (Oh Lord) are you so upset with me, for wanting you all to myself? For, I as well as you can see, I will never be able to fit in with those who have come after me. Surely, this you can feel now that you've shown your face upon me that I might know only you. Thus, now to be placed in a place that both you, and I know was created for the mere pleasure of you wanting to see a smile from me. Well, of me that's a no can do thing!

Now, like a shot in an instance. This voice of creation raised me up from his presence, and into the world that was the closest I was placed. Moreover, as I fell from this great and most wonderful presence, and down towards this world of calamity, chaos, and conflicts. I knew that the worst was yet to come. For I had displeased my father, and my Lord. However, this was not my intent. I mean, could he not see that I was happy with just him and me, for he was all I alone needed. But of course, somehow, I had failed in the conveying of that to him or was it that I should have been more accepting of this gift of great wonder and favor.

For it is written that it is a sin to refuse a gift, specifically one given from the heart. This is known as the lack of gratitude sin. But for me to be the first one to commit this unholy. Well it must have been like a slap in the face of this most Highest of Highs, the Lord of all Lords My father, the most good and powerful God! However, at the same time I felt, he was not even considering what it was, which would make me content either. So, with that in mind, and while falling from his presents. I rejected everything I felt would make this Lord of mine happy and with joy over his choice of my creation.

Moreover, in that moment, I became the complete opposite of all that he was, and without remorse or regret! For in me, my heart had been hurt and hardened, like being ripped out without the surgery. Now, keep in mind that this whole thing was new to me and the Lord as well, this thing called life here on Earth. Why? Because I had for so long been with the Lord, and no one else. I mean, to be in the mist of people, and without the presence of my Lord and father was liken to that of a body without a head attached. Yes, in a sense, I was lost and lonely. For I had been cast into this world of vial and evil creatures; without even a thought of what I must have been going through at the time! Moreover, in my mind, I was going to get even, even if it killed the whole of creation to do so!!

Now, keep in mind that the father had much the same feeling as me. I mean, understand not only is he the great creator of the universe, the worlds, and life as well. It is a known fact that he is also, the great destroyer as well. But, at that time in my life I would have welcomed death, rather than live without him on this rock called Earth. Look, you've got to understand that this is my father. That which created me. Yet now, he just pushed me out of his presence over a gift? Okay, so I made a mistake like most kids do, and really was it so bad to just want him and no one else alongside, while confiding and conveying my ideas?

Thus, I had to come to terms with the concept or idea of what they mean, when it is said *"It is better to humor them with a lie, rather than to baffle them with the truth!"* I mean like who could have wrote this? Perhaps me or maybe the father through me, any who, this is something that must be explored further at another time.

But the fact still remains that had I known that very statement, when confronted with that great and wonderful gift. Then maybe things, would have been much different, rather than the way they are today!

Now, here is the turn around to this whole madness, for somehow the Lord must have (like me), come to terms with the situation much like I did. I mean, the power that this great, and most powerful entity this *"I AM"* holds in just one word, is beyond all knowledge.

Yet, he (this great entity) stilled the anger which he felt towards my answer, and for once I believe he felt my pain as well. Why? I don't know why. But I can speculate that if in fact, he is all things like it is written in the word. Then the DNA for empathy, is also written into his design as well. Making him also, an empathic entity.

An entity truly able to take on the pains, and anxieties of all things great and small. For it is a known fact to know, is to understand that through the experience, and pain of others. Comes the hopes, and the solutions we know now as, "mercy and grace." So, with that line of thought. The only conclusion that can come from this, is that these are truly the actions of an empathic life force.

This is where the paradox comes into the equation, like just say for the moment. That this great gift, was not so much for me as it was for him. I mean, just think about how much he has evolved, and by coming to terms with the choice that I made on that day.

Look, had I not been as honest as I was, about what was in my heart towards the gift. Then perhaps he never would have ventured into his self, and touched with those hidden gifts, which lay within. Allowing him to share them, wholeheartedly through those creations which came after.

Like, could I have been the thing, which was created for just such a thing as this, and if so then what is the end pay off. I mean do I die, and go to the winds of time and space as recycled matter or do I gain the opportunity to in fact, be liken to that of a creator status, liken to that of a God!

However, if so what will be the greatest contribution that I can bring or contribute, which might keep the flow of this thing called creation evolving. So, in true retrospect, the paradox is empathy or grace and mercy. Plus, in return the only thing we have to do. Is to repent, and be humble along with having faith in the fact that there is a brighter light at the end of the road for all of us or all that seek, through these few small deeds that light at the end.

I truly urge you all to take the time, to feel the pain and anxiety, of those around you. Thus, for once, do what it might take to ease those pains and anxieties, which are found. For this in itself, is another way of finding out who or what you really are, in the eyes of the Lord as well…

~FOOT NOTE~

Had it not been for the truth and honesty, I showed that day; and regardless of the sacrifice or the consequence that followed. Perhaps the Lord may have never explored the paradox of empathy, and the world promised to me, might never have been built.

For now, more than ever. What I believe is becoming more and more, in view with what I see around me! That is, for one to be a creator of worlds and universes. One must have the qualities of all things both good and bad, along with the fact that you must also have the DNA code of empathy in your design as well. Meaning, you must be an empathic life force above all else.

Thus, the paradox becomes a statement of fact. Thank you, Lord Deity, for all that you've placed upon my plate. For when you really look at it, it's really not that full after all...

Kenneth Bernard Dean/LDD/Six (Author)

CHAPTER 8

Though I stand, still I've yet to Learn How to Walk

~A word from the Author~

The ability to stand does not always mean, the next move of the equation will generally be the art of walking, be it literally or spiritually yet the fact is, for every action there will be an apparent reaction. Thus even though understanding this to be the purest of the checks and balance system, which shall test man and woman's, ability to choose wisely a truer system and one that is better known to us as, "The option of choice factor in life," shell be the somewhat spark in both the man along with the woman that will motivate a since of a true cause. One that will dictate the course of their lives in either a life of Good or a life of Evil. They also will find this time in life to be the most revealing of their ability to react positively when confronted with the "art of choice" between the two stimuli's, "Pride and Faith." Yet, moreover we still find it to be very hard to choose favorably (for some of us) when faced with the only two stimulants allowed, which are Pride, and the most important one of them all Faith. For they activate the stimulations of "the choice," be it of the Pride point of view or from a more spiritually felt "while incorporating the whole of your environment," Faith born view point. However, this to us is somewhat the Ying or the Yang, the Left or the Right, the Six or the Nine, and the ups or the downs of life or simply said, "In whatever direction you choose to travel within it," life that is.

(A True Statement of Prophecy: From LDD/Six)

However there is a certain order to all things, thus even when faced with making "the hard choice" between the two. For it is said that "If a man choose wisely and make that choice the way of his life's journey, then by his Faith alone he shell be saved to spend eternity with the Father, the Almighty God the true Deity. But he who waist his choice on Prideful things be it, Self-Pride or the Pride of Ownership still loses, for they are both not of wise choice. Though true they both have something vividly tangible to offer, yet the fact is that because they are both not based on "True and Simple Faith," their longevity is of a very short existence.

Now in saying that in words, I hope to trigger the thing inside us all, you know that fear which forces a search within you "the reader" of said piece, and myself for the truth. Thus I challenge you, with an open mind and grace filled heart, supported along by your faith "to for just a short moment after the read", consider what is now your thoughts of these two concepts: the first one being "To be a Man one must first stand, for then and only then will he be able to walk the way of men up right and direct", and the second one "To be a True Man one must align his self through faith, and with the open knowledge of the infinite creator the Lord our Creator, the Almighty God the true Deity. For then and only then, will he find himself among those who will walk forever throughout eternity, and throughout the none-ending of time itself with that true Deity, the Lord the Almighty God our Father. Now with that said, I find myself confronted with the question of "Though I stand, still I've yet to Learn How to Walk," and what direction should I travel in towards finding the answer. Should I choose Pride, or do I choose Faith, this is a choice which is truly the equation that I must find the sum or answer too. For it is the answer to the type of life, be it "Good or Evil" which shall come from the choice made. However never forget that what one sees through their eyes, is sometimes not what truly is; because even those two stimuli "Pride and Faith" come with many faces to be considered when seeking the truth; so with no further ado, I give you the piece "Though I stand, still I've yet to Learn How to Walk" and like always I trust that you the reader will enjoy it...

Since I became aware of the meaning of the words which were being used in the conversations spoken to me, as well as what exactly they were saying over and over to me, since I first opened my eyes on the day of my birth some years ago. One thing or statement always puzzled me when it was spoken to me, and that was the statement *"Stand up and walk like a man,"* but what truly does that mean in all actuality. I mean does it simply mean to just get up and walk or does it have an even deeper meaning to this thing we know to be life, and if so how do I find this so called *"deeper meaning"* thus I began to look for the elusive reason behind that direct statement in the hope of finding the so called *"elusive deeper meaning."* Now in doing so, I found myself often in question over the choices that I made in life, while in search of that particular answer to that particular statement of *"Stand up and walk like a man."* Moreover the two most important stimuli, which are *"Pride and Faith"* which we use too activate the need for the use of the *art of choice,* sometimes left me also in question of whether or not I made the wiser of the choices throughout the whole of my life during those times when the *"art of choice"* had to be implemented.

I mean keep in mind, though my life is not one to be considered in the running as a contender for poster life of creation, it is still something that I shall find my thoughts captured by, like being under a spell, leaving me unable to either move from it or to even disregard the thoughts that it incurred upon this 'my wondering search' for the truth. However the fact that life operates on the results governed through the choice between, the two most basic *stimuli/emotions* which are *Pride and Faith,* is truly the ultimate *Constance.* Some might even say that the end results of a person's choice between the two, *Pride and Faith, is what constitute what is Evil and what is Good in the end. But keep in mind that what one see through their eyes in many cases is not what it is truly, and that also is a Constance!*

"For if it be that a man should have to kill to live, and that choice was based on the Faith that bonded him to his Creator, the Lord and true Deity, then regardless if all the Judges the world over judged him to be guilty, in the eyes of the Creator his innocence shell shine like the brightness of a star, for it is thus a "Just and Good deed" in the eyes of the Father the Lord the Deity. However if a man takes a life, and the choice was based purely out of Pride, and ownership moreover let's say he gets away with it. Then I would say that the works of that man was Evil, and though he may think he got away with the crime, he has yet to be judged face to face by his Creator, the Almighty God the true Deity."

Now the reason for those two scenarios is merely because they are both very extreme versions of the same situation, the taking of a life. *Nonetheless when you look at it closely, the Constance is always the choice between just two stimuli, "one a choice based on Pride or the other a choice based on Faith;"* the same two stimuli's that though they seem to be exact in their implementation and end results, they are still considered to be soft emotions, thus it is only fitting that they would be the basic emotions and/or choices which would determine your route through life be it good or evil. For you see the end results really do depend on what your choice is, and at every given time of your life when a choice has to be made. In some ways when you really look at it all, it becomes a rather large amount of responsibility through true knowledge (a knowledge which we have to first understand), and next through trying to use that same knowledge when confronted with choosing between those two stimuli's *Pride and Faith* each and every time in life, with the belief that each choice was the right choice, because keep in mind that your whole eternal life with the Father really does depend on it too be the right one.

Yet there is still the question of do Pride ever play a positive roll, and I would have to answer with yes. For it is not wrong to have Pride in your Creator the Lord Deity, the Almighty God. It is not wrong to have Pride in the work you do or the care that you give to those around you, be it physical or in kind. It is not wrong to have Pride in caring for the

Planet and the life forms that inhabit it for those alone are a few right off the top of my head.

Also the question has been raised, is it ever a time when Faith proves not to be positive or a Good thing, and of course I would have to say again, yes! For it is a bad thing for one to have Faith in the evil works of oppressive people as well as to have too much Faith in organizations which market the word merely for financial gains. It is also a bad thing when you, put the Faith that should be for the Creator into Mans tangible shortgevity, in the hope of finding heaven here in this Hellhole that we all worked so hard to build. Moreover that also came right off the top of the head, why because that is our true reality as well as nature.

Thus we find ourselves like lambs herded for the slaughter with the Faith that this is all just and right, thus we allow ourselves to be enslaved to those who (to themselves), would be Gods. But to me it is all Bullshit, for I know that the only one that can give me hope, forgiveness, love, life, favor, and when the time comes a peaceful transition; that existence in time commonly known to be called death, is the one who both Created me, and then from his own lungs blew life's air into me that I may have life, and that entity is known to me as the true Deity, the Almighty God Himself.

For it be of and too that power alone that I appeal too for the answer, now to some that may seem a little crude, and improper for a person to overlook those who would be called messengers of God. But it is a known fact that too trust man with your eternal future, is like putting your own head down a garbage disposal while turned on, hoping for good results, it just don't happen. Thus for me the only way is the "direct source way" for the true answers, and that would be to appeal to the Lord the Deity, the true Creator of us all for his truth, his answer.

Moreover, I have seen the works of man upon other men and know it to be the works of non-compassion, pain, deception, and finally death geared solely to feed that need to be him a god. Now to those who feel me to be somewhat arrogant, based solely off what they have read so far, I suggest that perhaps you might want to stop now, for what is to come may be a little too hard for you to stomach faith wise, but again that is really up to you if you continue.

So while sitting and gazing over my past life, there was something that just kept coming to the surface of all my thoughts, and it kept me in question as to if through the whole of my life, *"were the choices I made in the act of survival the best for me at that time. Moreover, had I not made them (the choice that is), would I still be here writing this piece now or would the life that I exist in be a long gone ordeal. Also does the fact that I am a survivor, based off the choices made, constitute that I have at least accomplished the ability to stand and walk like a man in the eyes of those around me"* and really do they even matter? These four questions somehow hit me like a ton of bricks, and for the first time in my life I was baffled as to what the answer may turn out to be. So for the many nights that followed, the Lord allowed me to (while in a somewhat state of slumber) revisit those moments when it was necessary for me to make those choices, as a spectator. Nonetheless as I viewed my past, it became clear to me that had I not made those choices, surely I would not be here today.

For it somehow became clear to me that the majority of the choices that I made were faith born ones, and even that startled me because I was under the belief that they were of a pride born need, and thus I would have to answer to them come judgment time. Nonetheless I was surprised of the fact that throughout the whole of my life, and because of the hard choices that I was forced to make for my survival, I had been catapulted into man hood long before I should have been. Sort of like the mind of a fifty year old man in the brain of a child under ten years old.

I mean my belief was that to be a kid was to have fun and learn step by step the rights to manhood, not overnight become a man just to survive. I mean there were no school sports or evening school plays to rehearse for. There was only anger and despair, hardships and thoughts of suicide; for it was clear that for many (the world over) liken to me, fun would never be a part of our childhood agenda. *For it had become clear that the road to happiness for our kind was to die with the hope for a better life next time around. But the Lord the Deity, would not hear of it, and for a while it became clear that perhaps it was necessary that I go through this thing (my life) for the amusement of the Lord the Deity, for that entity alone designed, and created me for his purpose and pleasure along, and no one else not even* me has the right to not except that as a true Constance or Fact in the true order of things! However it is wise to say like it has been said earlier, in the read that the purpose of man *(by way of his choosing deception as his tool)* is to convince those among, and around him as well as even himself that he *(somehow through the Darwin theory of design and natural order)*, has in fact evolved into the God we so should serve for our very existence here, and in the flesh or in this reality.

But even the blind over a period of time can see the lie for what it is, *"a lie of the worst kind."* Yet they are still willing to through their deceptive nature convince you to, through the implications of *the art of your choice between those two stimuli's (Pride and Faith), to align with them in this their final endeavor towards their goal or quest towards the unlikely God ship they so sort after with vast promises of "Wealth and Power to those who bow down before them, and take their mark; but what they don't tell you is that the price of punishment for such an act far outweighs the rewards of man, and are eternal in its Consequences and Nature".* I mean *does it really matter if you're the richest Rapper, Movie Star or greatest Sports Figure to date. Moreover the line between Corporate Ideology, and the Spiritual Ideology has become blurred plus so many are caught up by it, you know this fear of where do I go to from here thing!* For when the time comes the question that you will have to answer is the same one that I'll have to give answer to as well, thus I say to you and the many others who excepted the mark and that question is, for whatever the reason was or is it really worth the loss of eternity that you sale yourself to the one, even though he may have knowledge of some of the truth, yet still he market or make wager of your eternal soul with the promised lie of longevity, which come the time of judgment will no longer be anymore, for in that moment you also shell be no more as well. So again I ask, is it truly worth a future of eternity, gone like so little smoke among the breath of the voice of the Lord the Deity himself, the Almighty God or will you stand by your faith that in the end, the truth will be revealed?

Yet as I look around, it becomes vividly clear that there are still many among you, who continue to your right to the *art of choice* which is triggered by your *misuse* of the two most important stimuli's or emotions, *"Pride and Faith"* while never even considering the weight they carry in the final application of the decision of the end from either when chosen. Look the truth is that you have to face the facts that the recruitment part of the plan is working in over time, and the pitch is being delivered through *"reality television and the marketed word of a large number of the houses of worship among the many denomination gifted unto us by the father."* Thus the prophecy of the last book where it speaks clearly to the point that among the last days, many will be forced to run away and into the mountains where they can hold true to their belief while awaiting the return of the Deity, the Almighty God is real. For those are the time when those who refuse the mark, well they will be hunted and either they will be forced to take the mark or be destroyed. Now the thing that really should freak you out is the fact that today is the day, and the majority of the bounty hunters will be people who truly believe in God but, which one will they see when they finally open their eyes and look.

Is it the true and all loving Deity, the Lord the Almighty God or man on his throne unlike so many (want to be Gods) of the past. I mean though the facts are in your face, you still fall on bended knees before these *"liars and want to be or need to be Deities"* nonetheless it would be frightening had for it not being so repulsive. I mean all those souls like so much coal shoveled into a steam engine only to be transformed into fading smoke, never again to have form or solid existence throughout the none ending of time. So even again I must ask the question, since the lines between *"Corporate, and Spiritual Ideology"* has become blurred and man himself feels confident in his endeavor at being God on Earth, thus finally aligning himself with the knowledge of the dark arts or that which is commonly known as the gift of the fallen angels.

Truthfully I ask, do you really want to put the trust of your eternal future in the hands or on words of man, (*a most deceptive creature*) or would you rather trust the direct source knowing fully that in doing so, it is of your true *Faith and much love of Pride for the true Deity the Lord the Almighty God himself that the choice be made.* Now upon understanding all of this and how important something like *"the art of choice"* which is triggered by one of the two simple yet major stimuli's *"Faith and Pride"* and with the direct, and the most powerful *weight of the Consequences ever to be considered as the end results by either of them*. It truly becomes vital that I make those decisions alone plus be willing to face up to and answer for them (the choices that is). For if nothing else, at least one thing that I know is that in doing it that way, it allows me to be more responsible for my own gift the soul he trusted me with, and whether good or evil the life that he also trusted me with till such time I go before and present it to the *"Lord and his Council for examination and judgment"*, to which I ask that I might, in that moment, fine him to be in all his glory very merciful and filled with favor for me in that time of my great homecoming experience.

Moreover if at no other time at least one thing will be clear, and that is on that day, and in that moment the concept of *"Though I stand, I've yet to Learn How to Walk"* becomes a living prophecy now to be history, and with that I bid you fair well with the words "peace be with, and upon you while on your journey through this life known to be the test of trials and tribulations" or in another word, be firm in your personal relationship with the Father the Lord, and true Deity the Almighty God. Pretty much just do you and nobody else for the true purpose of your responsibility is the salvation of your own soul and no one else at this point in the game now, amen!!!…

~FOOT NOTE~

Yesterday Dr. Maya Angelo was called to be with the Lord the true Deity the Almighty God, and though many will find it to be a loss for we who are still here. I can only remind you than in time all that came from the Lord shall in time return, for that in itself is our true purpose the birth, the death, the judgment for in true nature that is the reality, the facts plain and simple. However my question to you is, when you look back on your own life and the choices that you made, triggered by the stimulants Faith and Pride can you be certain that they were the choice made positively towards a life of Good or made negatively towards a life of Evil, for that is something that should be most important to you at this point in the game. I mean it is imperative to anyone who seeks to be humbled by the Glory of the true Deity the Lord the Almighty God that this self-evaluation be done, like checking the three credit scores to see if in fact you qualify to buy that new car or home, but so much more important. For this self-evaluation will determine if in fact you qualify for an eternal place within the house of the father the Lord the Almighty God.

Understand just like an evaluation of you credit scores, which gives you the opportunity to fix whatever you must (credit wise) towards that new car or home, it is even more important that you do a self-evaluation of your life allowing you the opportunity to fix or repair your soul, guaranteeing you a place in the house of the Lord our Father, the Almighty God. Now this might seem too many to be of an individualized or selfish nature, but the fact is that when you work hard at repairing your own soul then the light about you become much brighter like that of a guiding light or inspiration to other seeking a way out of the darkness of life deceptions, thus allowing the opportunity for those others who are lost like once you were.

Again thank you for the time you took in reading this piece "Though I stand, still I've yet to Learn How to Walk" in the hope that something positive you gained from it, also like always I hope it gave you some joy as well…

Kenneth Bernard Dean/LDD/Six (Author and Scribe)

www.ingramcontent.com/pod-product-compliance
Lightning Source LLC
Chambersburg PA
CBHW021128130626
46554CB00002B/918